PALEO BY SEASON

A Chef's Approach to Paleo Cooking

PETER SERVOLD

Photography by Sarah Servold · Foreword by Diane Sanfilippo

VICTORY BELT PUBLISHING INC.
Las Vegas

First published in 2014 by Victory Belt Publishing Inc.

ISBN 13: 978-1-628600-06-3

Printed in the USA

RRD 0114

CONTENTS

To Grandma and Tom

FOREWORD

BY DIANE SANFILIPPO

New York Times bestselling author of
Practical Paleo and *The 21-Day Sugar Detox*

Photo by Michelle Lange

It's become easier and easier to step away from the kitchen and grab ready-made food on the way home from work, or pop a frozen, boxed meal into the microwave and call it dinner. Our lives are busier than ever, and yet there's something missing from our ever-Internet-connected days: connection—to our friends, to our families, and, yes, to our food. See, while we've made it so effortless to get food on the table, we're missing out on far more than the process of shopping for and preparing food. We're missing out on the connection that comes from gathering around a table to enjoy the food we've made with those we love.

Why am I talking about our connection to one another in the foreword to a cookbook? Well, if there's one thing I've learned in my years of friendship with Peter and Sarah Servold, it's that the connections we make around the table—whether at a post-Thanksgiving Saturday brunch of remixed leftovers or over breakfast at a rental home on vacation—nothing brings people together like food.

But a take-out pizza or cartons of Chinese food aren't going to do what a richly layered, flavorful soup or your home-cooked braised pork shoulder will. Something happens when a person—or group of people—spends time chopping, seasoning, and preparing a home-cooked meal that literally puts love into the food.

Now, I know what you may be thinking: "But I'm not *that* good of a cook! Who wants to gather around a table for my food?!" Well, in *Paleo By Season*, Chef Pete has you covered. He walks you through the concepts behind the cooking, with details on how to prepare yourself *and* your kitchen and tips for making it all just a little bit easier. We avoid being in the kitchen simply out of fear of what may result from the time spent there—that it may, perhaps, even be (gasp!) inedible. We've all been there, even Chef Pete, and our mistakes are part of the journey to becoming sufficient, efficient, and confident in the kitchen.

If there's one thing I've learned about Pete and Sarah, it's that they care very, very deeply about putting the freshest local and sustainably grown food on your table as often as humanly possible. Their passion for making the highest quality food more accessible—and for supporting the hard work of local farmers—shines in everything they do. From their impeccably sourced meal business, Pete's Paleo, to the lessons in this book about how to use everything from carrots and onions to romanesco and black trumpet mushrooms, Pete's motivation to get you comfortable with every ingredient in your kitchen shines through.

What *Paleo By Season* will teach you, beyond how to gain kitchen confidence, is one of the topics I'm asked about most: what the heck to do with the new-to-you seasonal veggies that arrive once you've bitten the bullet and signed up for your local organic farmer's CSA (community supported agriculture) box. With recipes organized by season and seasonal produce charts broken down by region, this book lets you know what to expect in the months ahead from your own CSA box (or local farmers market, farm stand, or grocery store). And, with Chef Pete's advice, you'll soon know how to prepare those less-familiar vegetables and fruits (and even cuts or types of meat) based on what you may already know quite well about similar foods. Even if you're not venturing into the world of community supported agriculture, you'll be enlightened on your regular trips to the grocery store and able to bring home something new and in-season and whip up a fantastic meal, thanks to what Chef Pete has served up in *Paleo By Season*.

INTRODUCTION

This book is about learning how to use seasonal ingredients while following a Paleo diet. To do this, though, you need a solid knowledge base of techniques.

As a chef, I don't really think too much about recipes. From day one in culinary school, it was drilled into me to use cooking methods, flavor profiles, and techniques to handle any and all ingredients, in any kitchen, anywhere in the world.

That being said, recipes are a really good starting point for learning techniques. It's often easiest to learn by doing, and there's no faster way to pick up a new technique than by cooking a recipe that uses it. The recipes in this book include instructions for some basic and many advanced techniques, so you'll be able to use those techniques again and again moving forward.

When your approach to cooking is driven by technique, you can go to your farmers market or open up that CSA box without trepidation or fear, knowing that whatever that box or market may hold, you've got the skills to turn it into something delicious. And whether you're a home cook or restaurant chef, letting what's on sale at the farmers market decide what you're making for dinner means you're always working with fresh, local, in-season ingredients, which make for the best meals.

And at the end of the day, that is the definition of Paleo: using what's available, when it's available, from the closest source possible. Driving to three different stores to find golden beets when the first store had parsnips, rutabaga, and turnips is just not Paleo. As a chef, I don't have time for it, and my guess is neither do you.

This book offers many recipes that you can follow to a T to make beautiful, flavorful food, but my goal is get you shopping and cooking like a Paleo chef. There are tons of maps and infographics to help you find what is in season in your area, and what substitutions you can make when something isn't in season or available.

My hope is that over time, you will become more and more comfortable with the techniques explained in the recipes, which will let you become less dependent on particular ingredients, so you can cook with whatever looks fresh and delicious at your farmers market. In short, you will learn to think like a Paleo chef.

AS YOU GO THROUGH THIS BOOK, FOLLOW THESE RULES

- **Have fun.** Taking time to cook for yourself and your family is one of the best returns on investment I've ever found. So enjoy the process.

- **Make mistakes.** Cooking is a process, and you will undoubtedly make mistakes. This, my friends, is a good thing—that's how you learn. I remember every scallop I oversalted and every pan of vegetables I forgot about in the oven until they were only good for charcoal. It's how I keep from doing it again.

- **Taste everything.** I can't stress this enough. The difference between a restaurant with a great menu and cool vibe but so-so food and a place that blows your socks off is a kitchen full of cooks who taste everything as they go. Cooking is a craft, not an innate talent, and you'll get the best feedback from your own palate. Taste the food you're making as you go and learn not just when it needs a little more salt or a little less pepper (although that's important, too) but also how flavors and textures change over the course of the cooking process. This is so crucial to growing as a cook.

A WORD ON THE PALEO DIET

I am a chef. It's what I went to school for and how I make a living. I am not a doctor, nutritionist, or scientist. So I don't have much to say about why eating fresh, local, and in-season—eating Paleo, essentially—is good for you. There are plenty of people smarter than me who have already handled this quite well—like Diane, who you just heard from in the foreword. (Thanks, Diane.) In my family, we have found that by eating properly sourced meat and seasonal produce, we are living quite healthy by all measurable markers. The food tastes pretty damn good, too.

DIFFICULTY LEVEL

Below the ingredients list for each recipe, you'll find colored dots indicating the recipe's difficulty level.

● These recipes require little time and effort to execute. You should be able to bang them out with relative ease and have them in your back pocket wherever you go.

●● These foods are pretty easy to make, but they require lots of cooking time and therefore a little more planning. There won't be too much knife work or any crazy techniques, however.

●●● Three dots! Whoa, things are getting serious. These recipes call for more knife and prep work and some techniques that may be new to you, and they have a necessary emphasis on planning ahead and having your *mise en place* together.

●●●● Welcome to my world. These are fine-dining Paleo recipes. They require a thorough read-through and adherence to the game plan that's been laid out. This food is for impressing yourself and your guests with what you can do in the kitchen. Don't even tell them it's Paleo; just blow them away. Have fun.

WHY I COOK,
AND NOW COOK PALEO

You probably picked up this book assuming that it's focused on the seasons because seasonal eating is a wonderful way to eat local, healthy, flavorful food. And you were right. Seasonal eating is, to me, the only way to really appreciate fresh produce and the bounty of the earth—the only way to eat, really.

Everybody has their story, though, and how I got to Paleo and came to write this book is shared below. I hope you see some common ground in our goals for healthy, seasonal eating and healthy, happy lifestyles. Thanks for reading.

My first food memories are of making meatballs with my grandma at her house in Ledyard, Connecticut. We would measure all the ingredients out together, and my favorite part was mashing it all together with my hands, feeling all the squishiness. Squishiness is underrated. I remember trying to make a perfectly shaped meatball every time and glancing up to see if it got Grandma's approval before putting it on the sheet pan, lining it up with the rest in a perfect row. I couldn't have been much more than five or six.

It was in these times—reveling in the smells, the colors, the process, always the process—that I fell in love with food.

When I was in fourth grade, I ran home from school every day to watch *Great Chefs of the World*, which featured an appetizer, an entrée, and a dessert, each prepared by a different great chef from around the world. The way they worked was so beautiful. They were methodical, organized, and prepared. I began to notice some constants: salting and sometimes peppering throughout the cooking process, clean work stations, everything within arm's reach, and concise, efficient movement. Once I saw a chef make a perfect quenelle one-handed, and it blew my mind. I learned early on that I have a propensity to be a huge dork about certain things.

But could I cook? My first attempt was a disaster. I made stuffed chicken breast for my parents. I'm still haunted by this dish, which I made with raw spinach and raw mushrooms (never, ever, ever do this) and cooked in the oven for two and half hours. Perfect, assuming I was trying to discover how they dehydrate and pulverize chicken for dog food.

Luckily for me, the ability to not give up when you completely destroy a dish is a necessary trait for eventually figuring it out.

When I graduated from high school, I was excited to be admitted to a program that would let me study restaurant and hotel management during the morning and take PGA lessons and turf management classes in the afternoon. Essentially, it gave you a degree in running a resort, country club, or hotel. It was perfect for me, and I was devastated when I got a call that my spot in the program had been given away to someone with a better handicap, or GPA, or something like that. I wasn't really listening.

After a brief, unfortunate stint at Arizona State University, I began to drift. For many reasons, almost all imaginary, my life became about drinking. My parents moved us too much; I was too smart for the people around me and needed to dumb myself down; my girlfriend didn't get me; whatever. My life had never been farther from good health and cooking than it was over those next few years.

I moved to Germany for awhile. The beer is good there, I can confirm that, and after a series of other questionable decisions I moved to Madison, Wisconsin, where I found out that if you want to have someone to drink with anytime, day or night, a college town is the place for you.

Fortunately Madison is also a good place to meet smart, ambitious people, and one of them changed my life. Dan Tefera, an economics professor who had received his PhD from the University of Wisconsin, was opening an Ethiopian restaurant with his partner, Yeshi, and hired me as a server. I instantly fell in love with working in a restaurant. I loved all the new flavors of the Ethiopian food, I loved learning the language, the buzz of a busy dining room, the dirty dishes stacked efficiently in the sink, and I loved going out after a crazy shift on a Friday night with my work buddies.

The restaurant life was hard, but it involved working with my sort of folks, it suited my kind of lifestyle (mostly the high level of alcohol and drug use), and I was pretty good at it. Life was fun and I loved my work, but my demons were still there. I could never get enough of partying.

Looking back, I can see that many people, many times tried to get me to ease up, but I was just oblivious.

Then one day my dad called and said he had retired from his decades-long career with Mc-Donald's. He planned to open a wine and cigar store in Atlanta and wanted to know if I would help. For all my faults, when family calls, I will always be there.

But it didn't go as planned; one wine store was just too small for the personalities of my brother, dad, and myself. I continued to work at the store for three years off and on and learned an incredible amount about wine, people, and running your own business. But it wasn't going to work in the long run. I started waiting tables at a barbecue place up the street. The chef was awesome, classically trained, and he gave me a copy of Michael Pollan's *The Omnivore's Dilemma*. My mind was blown.

Most people who read a book that sparks in them passion, anger, interest, and love, would make a game plan to make its message a part of their life. I thought it was a great reason to be angry and drink more. I was arrested for driving under the influence. I was very lucky I didn't kill myself or, worse, someone else. That's kind of the boilerplate response, but it's true. I'm horrified when I think about my past behavior. I've learned a lot from that time, including but not limited to: never do it ever again.

During this period of destruction I somehow managed to go to culinary school. It was a tough couple of years, but I graduated and got the job of a lifetime at Restaurant Eugene in Atlanta. It's there that I learned everything you're holding in your hands.

I was using the best ingredients from the best sources and working with the best chefs in the city. It was incredible: We would cook for Robert Duvall one night and *Bon Appétit* editors the next, always making everything from scratch. We made the bread, the ketchup, the mustard, the marmalade; we butchered the whole animal, made the pepperoni, ground the burger, cured the duck bacon. Everything was done in-house.

After a year I left Restaurant Eugene to make more money slinging eggs at a breakfast place. It felt wrong, but financially, it was necessary. Then I went on to bartending and waiting tables at a bar. More dark times were forecast, until I met the last beautiful woman I'll ever meet in my life.

I met Sarah when she came into the bar where I was working in June 2010. We were introduced through mutual friends, and I couldn't take my eyes off her. We ate fish jaw and cow brains on our first date and I was in love. I mean, she's a Yankees fan, but I was still in love.

Shortly after I met Sarah, a terrifying bout of pericarditis—inflammation of the pericardium, the sac around the heart—left me sick and scared that, if the doctors were right, it would happen again and again throughout my life. After that, it didn't take much cajoling from Sarah to get me to start doing CrossFit with her. I loved it; still do. But then she wanted to do something called Whole30 that had something to do with this Paleo thing.

At first, I agreed mostly in an effort to make the hot girl happy. Even after my brush with heart pains, I was not crazy about the idea of not eating rice, or butter, or cream, or cheese—though the real issue was, no alcohol! I mean, sure, I had some issues, but we had just started dating, and that's a tough time to not have any liquid courage.

But then something pretty great happened. In learning about Paleo and all the things you can eat, I was inspired. Paleo is fine dining. You go to the farmers market, get whatever is local and in season, and make it for dinner. There is absolutely no difference between that and what we do in a nice restaurant. Well, there was one difference: in the restaurant, we make it taste good. Most of the Paleo recipes I saw were pretty run of the mill, and while Sarah and I were eating better than we had in our entire lives, most people were eating grilled chicken and steamed broccoli.

That's how the idea for Pete's Paleo was born. It would "bring fine dining to your cave" by combining the techniques and sources of a fine restaurant with the convenience of ready-to-eat meals. We moved to San Diego in November 2011, got married in December, and in February 2012 we started the company with the savings left over from our wedding. I cooked for two clients out of the little kitchen in our Ocean Beach cottage. Now we do a few thousand meals a week.

Things have changed quite a bit for us over the past two years. My life has just begun in a lot of ways. Our business is growing and presenting us with more opportunities every day, all of which we are infinitely grateful for. You're reading this book. Sarah is carrying our first child—little Lois Marie will be here towards the end of June. I'm only mildly terrified, which I think means it hasn't really sunk in yet.

Things can change and get better, if you help them get better. And a great place to start is with the stuff that fuels your existence as a human being, otherwise known as food.

Care about it, learn about it, take time making it. Not much can go wrong with learning how to make whole, real food from scratch with and for your family, and a whole lot can go right. I'm not unique. Anyone who begins to make positive changes in their life will see dividends beyond what they expected, much faster than expected.

But of course you have to start! Everybody starts working out and eating better on the same day: tomorrow. Pick up your damn knife, turn off *Keeping Up with the Kardashians*, take your kid to a farm, move. Because at the end of the day, that's what is always so great about food—it's real, rewarding work. Even if we lived in a utopia, carrots would still have to be peeled and brisket would need to braise for quite a while.

Make mistakes, cut your finger, burn your arm and the pork chop. I've learned my greatest lessons with my biggest screw-ups, in life and the kitchen. In both arenas, get started today.

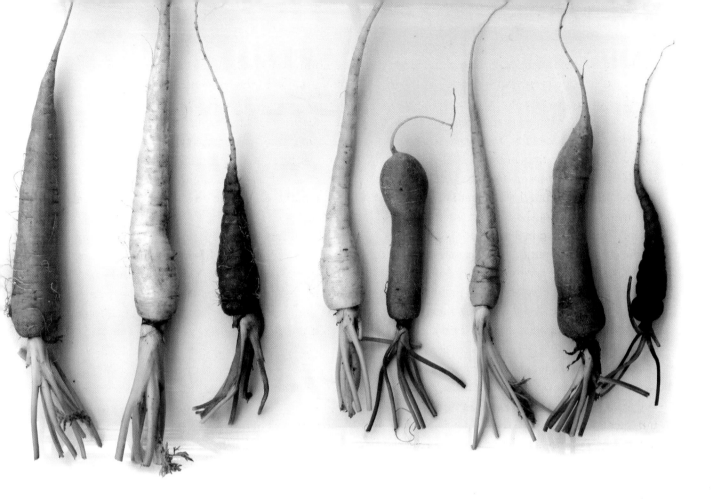

COOKING TEMPERATURES

These recipes were tested on a home stove with gas burners and no convection. That being said, even if you have the same setup, there may be differences. Your burner may emit a different number of BTUs (heat energy) than mine, or your oven may get hotter than what it says. (It's a great idea to use a separate oven thermometer to calibrate your oven, so you know where it really ends up when you set it to 350°F.) If you have an electric stove with a glass top, you've probably already noticed that it tends to take awhile to cool down once it heats up.

All of these things need to be taken into account when cooking. If the instructions say to warm up the pan for two minutes on medium-high heat and that makes your pan smoke, then turn the heat down or warm it for a shorter period of time.

As you cook the recipes in this book, think about what you're working with and why you're using a certain technique. After making a few recipes you will figure out what adjustments you need to make, much as you know a 32 waist in one brand is a 30 in another.

HOW I COOK

It's one thing to work your way through a handful of recipes and make dinner for yourself and your family; it's another thing entirely to not take all day to do it. In a restaurant, chefs get to the kitchen between noon and 1 p.m. and spend four to five hours getting the stations prepped and ready for dinner service. It takes about ten to fifteen minutes to "fire" a plate, which is when we get an "order in" and it's ready to be made. In a typical service on a busy night at our restaurant, we served about 150 diners in three hours. There were roughly twenty-five items on the menu, each of which was composed of at least four and up to nine components.

The techniques I honed in a busy restaurant kitchen in order to do all this can help you to be organized and prepared at home, too. First, let's take a look at an example of what was coming off my station, the hot apps station:

- butternut squash soup, toasted spice pecans, chive oil
- seared dry pack scallops, sunchokes two ways, pâte brisée, chowchow
- foie, toasted brioche, Muscat puree
- sweetbreads, pressed apple, duck egg, delicata squash puree, arugula pesto

This station was a big deal for me. Not only was it the first time they trusted me with a full set of burners, it was the second station on the line and came with more responsibility and prep. I really loved this station. I could sear scallops and sweetbreads all day and be content.

Before beginning to cook anything, it was crucial to list every step needed to make each dish. Here's the prep list for the menu above:

- split and roast butternut squash
- scoop out butternut flesh, sauté with onions, puree

- toast pecans, make pecan seasoning
- blanch / shock chives
- puree chives in oil / steep / strain
- clean scallops, pack in ⅓ pan with paper towels
- slice and fry 1 pound sunchokes for chips
- peel and clean 3 pounds sunchokes
- clean / steep sunchokes in heavy cream / strain / puree
- scale and mix pâte brisée / rest
- cut and bake pâte brisée
- chop all veg for chowchow / measure, boil liquid / steep
- clean and portion foie gras
- portion, cut, and toast brioche (don't burn it this time)
- boil Muscat grapes for 1 hour
- put boiled Muscat through food mill
- strain and puree Muscat pulp
- chop mirepoix for sweetbreads
- bread and fry sweetbreads, add stock and mirepoix
- cut apple / seal in sous vide bag
- gather duck eggs on station
- split and roast delicata squash, scoop out, and puree
- blanch / shock arugula
- dry arugula and make pesto
- chop shallots / garlic / parsley for station
- gather all finishing oils and vinegars / make fresh finishing oil if necessary
- gather all microherbs and final garnishes for all dishes and place on expo station

Photo by Bill Staley

Looking at this list can give me a mild panic attack even today. And you know what? This was a relatively easy station. The list for the entrée and roast station was twice as long. The only way to get all this done in a few hours is to work as efficiently as possible, and the way to do that is to plan out and consolidate the steps.

After looking at the menu as a whole and listing the prep tasks, we have wrapped our heads around what needs to be done, so now we need to know the how. I look at what takes the longest to prepare and cook.

When I walk in the kitchen, the first thing I (and most chefs) do is get some water boiling and turn the oven on at around 375°F. You will invariably need boiling water for blanching at some point, and while the oven may need to be slightly higher or lower for your particular needs, getting it up around 375°F means that it is hot when you need it. Nothing is worse than chopping a whole case of vegetables to be blanched or roasted and realizing you never turned the oven on or got the pot of water on the stove.

So get some water on and get your oven going. Start with the foods that take the longest. Don't shave radishes and supreme oranges until the beets are already in the oven. Work smart, not hard. Whenever possible, get things done a day ahead of time, or cook basics in large batches and repurpose them throughout the week.

Write down all your dishes and their components, group similar prep tasks together, and get the grouped tasks done all at once—for instance, cut all the squash in half, then scoop out all the seeds, then toss all the squash in oil and bit of salt and put all of it in the oven at once. It's so much more efficient than cutting one squash, then scooping out the seeds, then tossing it in oil, and then moving on to the next squash. It's crazy how much faster it is to do each step for all ingredients instead of prepping each ingredient individually.

Have a game plan for your meals and your week. Think like a chef when you're looking over your CSA box and figuring out what to do for the week. (Tips and strategies for using a CSA box can be found on page 125.) Plan around nights when you won't have time to cook and make extra portions on the other days so you can still have home-cooked food. Prior preparation prevents piss-poor performance.

MUST-HAVE EQUIPMENT

You only need a few good pieces of equipment to stock a kitchen. Spend the money on quality items and they will last literally your entire life. Add them slowly, stocking up on birthdays and holidays.

KNIVES

It all starts with a good knife. One really good chef's knife is all you need for 95 percent of what you will encounter. Yes, there is a "perfect" knife for filleting a fish or deboning a chicken, but unless you're doing a hundred of them a day, a chef's knife will handle the job just fine. I prefer the Wüsthof brand. An 8-inch chef's knife in their Classic line is about $80 to $100. I have cooked 100,000 meals with a Wüsthof I got five years ago, and it's still awesome. I've also used and own a couple of very nice Japanese knives from Global, Glestain (pricey but beautiful), and Shun. Go to a kitchenware store and try holding several different knives to find one that works for you. The Global, for example, is very light and nice to look at, but the top of the blade is very thin, so if you're doing lots of heavy-duty work with butchery or cutting dense vegetables like winter squash, you're going to get a wicked callus in a hurry. Find a knife that works for you; on any given line in any given restaurant, every cook will swear by a different brand. All you really need to know is that you can't go wrong with any of the knives listed above. They are all of comparable quality, and what you use really is a matter of personal preference.

CUTTING BOARDS

Once you've put down a little bit of dough on the knife, you've got to spend a little bit more on a cutting board. No sense spending money on a good knife and then using it on a crappy cutting board. Wood is really the only way to go—the plastic boards are garbage, and glass is just stupid and dangerous. Boos blocks are the best, but they ain't cheap, and really any brand will do, unless someone else is buying. (Thanks, Joan and Neal, for my Boos block.) You can get a decent cutting board at any kitchenware store for around $50. The most important thing to look at is the thickness; a thick board will keep its shape and last longer. Store clerks will try to sell you wood conditioner—just rub it down with a tablespoon of olive oil after every wash and dry. Always dry it standing up and never let it sit on the damp towel you put underneath it to keep it from moving. (You do put a damp towel underneath it to keep it from moving, right? Good.)

PANS

Next on the list are a good cast iron pan and a good braising pan. I'm going to go out on a limb and say that these two things are pretty much all the cookware you need at home. Sure, you may want a nice egg pan for quick omelets and over easy eggs, or a heavy-bottomed sauté pan since the cast iron weighs ten pounds and is pretty hard to throw around. Besides that, though, these two are really all you need.

I don't know the science behind it, but nothing cooks better than cast iron. It gives you the perfect sear, perfect heat retention, and perfect one-pan cooking. I just love, love, love cast iron. And here's the best part: they're $20. Yeah, $20. They last, literally, generations. And their care is simple: just wipe out a cast iron pan with a paper towel and coat it with olive oil, and it's ready for the next use. Lots of folks have different seasoning methods; mine is to use it every day. Never, ever wash it with soap and water. If it gets dirty, scrape it with a spatula, wipe it with a towel, oil it, and use it again. Every day.

A good braising pan is thick, enamel-coated or copper, and coated with steel on the inside. Le Creuset is really the bee's knees here. Sure, they cost a couple hundred bucks and you can get comparable knock-off versions, but they just won't last like Le Creuset will. Like cast iron pans, they will last for generations. You can use them for making stews, braised greens, soups, and stock, and for sautéing and, of course, braising. We use them every day, every damn day.

FOOD PROCESSORS

Food processors are super useful and not nearly as expensive as they used to be. You can get a very decent one from Cuisinart for $50 to $100, depending on size and features. They are great for making burgers out of fresh meat, sauces, soups, salsa, dough for dumplings, mayonnaise, and hundreds of other things. It's one of those things that, once you have it, you'll never know how you lived without it. Put it on your Amazon wish list and treat yourself when your first thirty-day Paleo cleanse challenge is over.

INDUSTRIAL SHEET PANS

These are not the cookie sheets you are thinking of. These have a lip about an inch high and are sometimes called "jelly roll pans" for their use in manufacturing diabetes—I mean jelly rolls. They are made from aluminum and last forever. The best size for home use is what's called a "half sheet pan," 18 by 13 inches. You can get them online at Amazon for about $10. This is one of those things you really want to have the commercial version of. The cookie sheets you get at Target or Walmart are just a waste of time—they always bend and crack, and the coating on them never lasts. The commercial ones are a few bucks more and will last forever. They are perfect for roasting all the vegetables you could ever want and great for resting meat or finishing it in the oven. They are also great for loading up your prepped veggies or meat, like a portable prep table that you can also cook with. The sheet pan is something that's found in every restaurant kitchen, and you should add one to your home kitchen, too.

STRAINERS/COLANDERS

I really like a fine-mesh wire strainer. It's perfect for all kinds of foods and can be also used as a tamis. (You can push squash and other root vegetables through it to puree them if you don't have a processor or blender.) A small, handheld strainer is great for sauces or herb oils. Colanders are better suited for draining cooked vegetables in large quantities; they tend to be sturdier and have a foot base to hold them up.

THAT'S IT?

There are other items, of course. A nice blender like a Vitamix is great, an immersion blender is quite useful, and who doesn't want a good utility knife? But you'll never run out of things to cook with the above items. Need a meat mallet? Use the cast iron pan. Lids for pots? Use the sheet pans. Almost nothing in a kitchen is used for just one purpose. A single-purpose item in a kitchen is essentially useless. Add the items listed here over time, spending money to get the quality versions. Don't short-change yourself on these; you'll just be annoyed at how quickly the cheap versions break down and how poorly they perform.

KEEPING YOUR KNIFE SHARP

Sharpening my knife is meditation for me. There's something about connecting to our roots when we rub a piece of metal on stone to sharpen it. I feel like a Japanese sword master doing something that's been done for thousands of years. It's also not that hard to do at home, and three or four sharpenings a year is enough to keep your knives nice and sharp.

The honing steel, that steel dowel with a handle that came with your knife block, does exactly that—it hones; it does not sharpen. It pulls up the burrs and evens out the wear of the knife, but it does not give it a new edge the way a stone will. Use your honing steel every time you use your knife—just a half dozen swipes and you are set.

There are two types of sharpening stones: a tri-stone and a whetstone. The main difference is that the tri-stone has three separate stones of different grades while a whetstone has just one.

The coarser the grade, the more metal it's going to take off the knife with each pass, so the coarser stones should be used lightly. The finer the grain, the less effect it has on the blade with each pass.

Those three separate stones make a tri-stone a very bulky piece of equipment. It's great if you are sharpening a set of knives that have been left out for too long or have never seen a stone and are badly in need of sharpening. But if you have a good knife to start with or it's brand new, a medium-grade whetstone is all you need to keep it sharp for its lifetime. I tend to find the whetstone easier to use; it's also very easy to store and transport, and it's much less of an investment up front. I've had the same $50 whetstone for seven years and it still works great.

HOW TO USE A WHETSTONE

Put the stone in a pan full of water and let it soak for at least 20 minutes. Lay out a wet dish towel that's slightly wider than the stone. Remove the stone from the water and place it on the wet towel, keeping the pan with water nearby to rinse off the stone as you use it.

Holding the knife in your dominant hand, set it on the stone at a 45-degree angle with the handle at the bottom and tip at the top. Set the knife edge at a 15-degree angle to the stone, then pull the knife towards you while applying pressure with the fingers of your other hand on the side of knife. Run the knife diagonally across the surface of the stone to maximize surface contact. The sharpening motion is two-fold, a pull-and-push motion. The pull towards you sharpens the blade, then on the way back, the stone removes the burrs from the knife, evening it out.

Without taking the knife off the stone, push the knife back up in the opposite direction without applying any pressure (this would ruin the effort you made on the first pass). Continue the motion back and forth, pressing hard on the down pull and applying no pressure at all going back. After twenty to thirty back-and-forths, flip the knife over to the other side. Now apply pressure on the up slide and lighten pressure on the down. Again, make about twenty to thirty passes.

Take your honing steel and give it just a few slides down each side of the knife. You can test the sharpness by holding up a piece of paper and slicing through it. It should go through with relative ease and no sticking points.

This is another one of those things that you won't get perfect right away. Every knife brand has a slightly different angle to the edge, so some knives need to be sharpened at, say, a 12-degree angle and others at 16 degrees. Don't be discouraged if your first few attempts don't give you perfect results. Pay attention as you sharpen, using the "holding paper" test to judge which angle is best.

HOW TO BUTCHER
A CHICKEN AND FILLET A FISH

Learning to butcher a chicken or fillet a fish takes time. The first time I filleted a snapper in culinary school, I tore it to shreds—it would barely have qualified for cat food. But after six weeks of classes I got pretty good, and then after working at a seafood restaurant and butchering 200 pounds of fish a day, I got damned good. The point is that butchering, like cooking, is not some innate talent. It's a craft that takes study.

It may take six months to learn how to get all the meat off a chicken in one try, but after that, you'll be able to do it for the rest of your life. And you'll also find it's a skill that will carry over to duck, pheasant, quail, or any other poultry. They are all put together about the same. It's the same with that snapper—every fish has its quirks, but once you've got one down, the rest will come quite easily. How cool would it be to be the person who can break down the just-caught tuna on the boat during the fishing trip? Though don't try to do this and lose a thumb. Please.

Following are step-by-step instructions for butchering a chicken and filleting a fish. For the chicken, I will show you two ways: in the first, you take the breast off the bone and "airline" it; in the second, you leave it on the bone, which gives you a much juicier cooked breast. Both methods have their uses, as explained below. Don't expect to be great at the start, but know you'll get a little better every time you do it, and in a couple weeks or months you'll be quite good, and you'll have that skill forever. It's well worth the effort.

HOW TO BUTCHER A CHICKEN: OFF THE BONE AND AIRLINED

This method makes for a beautiful presentation of roasted breasts and wing meat. You'll need your trusty chef's knife, a big cutting board with a damp towel underneath to keep it steady, and a clean kitchen towel (don't forget to wash it as soon as you're done; raw chicken meat is full of bacteria).

Before you begin, use the clean kitchen towel to pat the chicken completely dry. You can also use it to hold the chicken as you work.

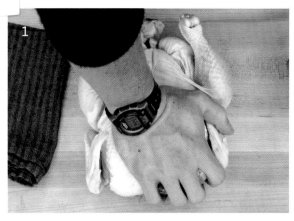

1 **Flatten the bird:** Place the bird on its back on a cutting board and push down on the breastbone until you hear a little pop. This flattens the bird and gives you better leverage throughout the butchering process.

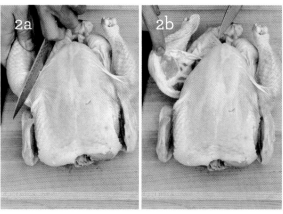

2 **Cut the skin at the leg:** Push the legs and thighs away from the breast and find the line of skin holding them together. You want to err more towards the thigh and leg when slicing into the skin, so that as much skin as possible is left on the breast. This both looks better in presentation and helps keep moisture in the meat. Gently slice through the skin while holding the leg and pulling it away.

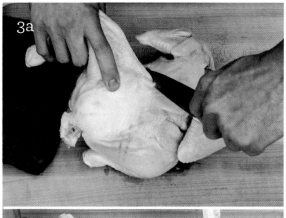

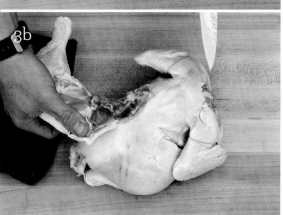

3 **Remove the oyster:** Work your way up and towards the chicken's back, rolling the chicken over as you go and keeping the leg pulled back towards you—you will hear a pop. Now comes the elusive oyster. To this day I still only get one out of two of these things completely. Look along the back and see where the thigh meets the backbone. You will see a little nugget of flesh just above where they meet. This is the oyster. You want to go up and around the oyster with the just the tip of the knife and try to scoop it out, then come back down the other side along the backbone.

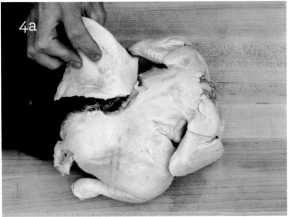

4 **Cut down to the thigh and leg:** From there it's a straight shot down to the bottom of the bird, where the thigh and leg will pull away in one piece. You can leave it whole or, if you prefer to separate them, use nature's perforation line: a line of fat on the inside of the thigh and leg. Put your knife directly on it and slice down. If you are struggling at all, you've missed; readjust slightly and you'll find it.

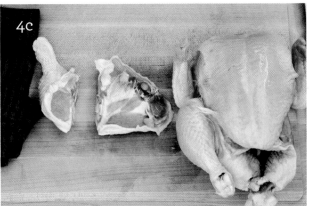

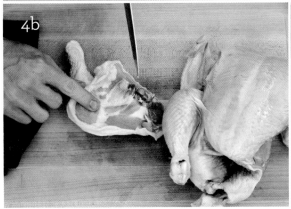

5 **Repeat on the other side of the bird:** You will find this side slightly easier or slightly more awkward depending on whether you're right- or left-handed.

6 **Cut away the breast:** Push down again hard on the breastplate and flatten the bird. Turn it so its top is facing towards you and put your knife directly on the center of the breastbone. Begin slicing downwards and the knife will find a side to start to come down on. Follow it along the inside of the breastbone, slicing towards you. Going a little deeper each time you slice, begin to pull the breast away as you go down. When you reach the ribs you can begin slicing sideways, following the rib bones, until you've pulled the whole breast off the bone.

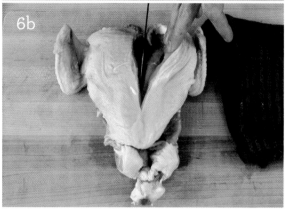

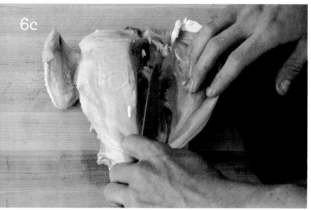

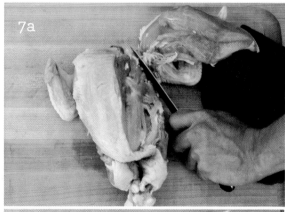

7 **Detach at the wing:** The breast will still be attached at the wing. Find the small gap between the wing bone and the rib cage and slice your knife through. The breast and wing are now free.

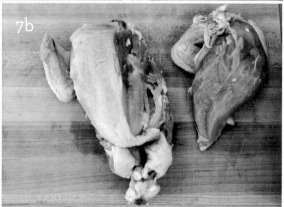

8 Cut away the wing tip: Slice at the first joint from the tip of the wing back, straight down through the bone. You can save the wing tip to add to the carcass for a stock. Old-school rules dictate cleaning the meat off the wing part still attached to the breast, but that's good meat right there, so I leave it on.

9 Repeat on the other breast: Flip the bird's tail towards you now and rotate as needed as you cut. Again, you will find this side slightly more or less comfortable depending on which is your dominant hand.

You have now butchered the chicken! Put the carcass in a stockpot for stock, or roast it and then make stock (see recipe on page 270).

HOW TO BUTCHER A CHICKEN: BONE-IN CHICKEN BREAST

Bone-in chicken pieces are best used for whole roasting and frying; they provide much, much better flavor.

For a bone-in chicken breast, follow steps 1 to 5 above and then, using a heavy santuko or chef's knife, put the bird on its "head" while holding on to the backbone. Starting at the inside of the bottom of the breast, cut down and through the rib bones until you come to the neck. You will find there are two joints on either side of the neck bone that need to be cut through to free the breast. Use the heavier edge of the chef's knife (the part closer to your hand) to push through these joints.

Next, take the breast and put it skin side down on the cutting board. With a very sure hand, place the knife dead center on the sternum of the chicken breast. Using your free hand, whack the top of the knife to pop through the breastplate. Once through, slice the breast in half. Take the wing off the bird by holding the breast up by the wing, slicing up towards the "armpit" of the breast, and letting gravity pull it apart. You now have a bone-in chicken breast.

This will not go as smoothly as written above the first few times. After three or four birds, however, you'll find your groove, and in short order you'll be a chicken butchering machine. Never again will you pay the ridiculous upcharge for separate chicken pieces, and you will always have bones on hand for stock and soup.

HOW TO FILLET A FISH

The fish we used for these pics is a beautiful red snapper from my boy Tim at Point Loma Seafood, an awesome fish market and counter service restaurant in my neighborhood in San Diego. You probably have one in your neighborhood, too, so go give them your money! (Or at least give them a try once, and if the fish is great and the proprietor seems to know their stuff, keep going.) Many local fish markets around the country are small and need the patronage of the neighborhood to stay open.

One of the great benefits of going to local fish markets is that you can find clues to the fishes' freshness; once it's gone to the supermarket and has been filleted and wrapped in plastic, it's harder to determine if a fish is really fresh. Look for fish that have deep red gills and clear eyes. Any off color or cloudiness in the gills or eyes is a no-no. It should smell fresh, like the water it came from, not "fishy" in a bad way. If you're feeling adventurous and you have a super-fresh ocean trout or salmon, rub your hand on the belly meat—it smells like watermelon. True story. There is a difference between a bad and good fish smell, and a good fishmonger will be able to show you.

What you'll need

- A cutting board bigger than the fish you are working with
- A damp paper or cloth towel underneath the board to keep it steady
- If you have one, a fish knife. They are shaped like regular boning or slicing knives but are slightly flexible, so it's easier to follow the contours of the fish. They're nice, but not necessary; I've broken down many more fish with a chef's knife.
- Two clean, lint-free kitchen towels
- Fish bone pliers (any small, spring-loaded, needle-nose pliers dedicated just for this purpose will do—it's a small and worthwhile investment)

1 **Place the fish on the cutting board:** Lay the fish down on its side. Watch your hands on its fins on the top and sides; they can sting and, if you're very sensitive, cause your hand to swell. If you are right-handed, lay the fish with its head towards the right side of the board; if you are left-handed, have its head at the left.

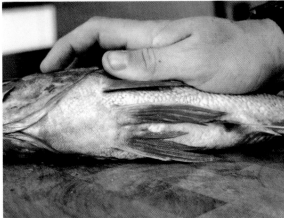

2 **Open the fish:** Carefully open up the fish's stomach if the fishmonger has not already done so. Don't go deep: use just the tip of the knife so you don't puncture the organs.

3 **Remove the organs:** Pull the organs out whole and discard. There are some folks who use the organs, but they are just way too strong for me. Have at it if that's your thing.

4 **Cut underneath the jaw:** Take one of your clean towels and wipe the fish down; it's gonna be a little slimy. Starting with your knife at an angle that's parallel to the backbone, and with the point positioned behind the fin at the bottom of the fish's jaw, gently slice down to the center bone, moving from the top downward to underneath the jaw.

5 **Make a shallow cut on the back:** Make a slight horizontal incision from the beginning of the first incision on the top of the fish down the backbone. You are making your guideline for taking the fillet off here. Barely breaking the skin, follow the top bone down to the tail of the fish.

6 Cut deeper into the fish: Now go back again towards the top of the fish where you began and make deeper cuts into the fish, pulling the fillet away as you go. Take care to only use the very tip of the knife, slicing just a little at a time. (You will get more confident and your movements smoother over time, but little mistakes here take big chunks out of the fish.)

7 Avoid the center bone: There is a troublesome bone in the dead center of the fish—you will have to go slightly up to get over it, then right back down. It is very easy and common to go up and through the fillet with your knife or down and into the fillet on the other side here. Don't despair, we've all done it.

8 Cut away the fillet: As you begin to get towards the end of the fillet, using the knife, follow the bones of the fish all the way down to the bottom of the belly and slice the fillet off.

9 Create a faux fillet: Flip the fish over, reversing the direction the head is facing. Now take the other towel, fold it to about the fish's size, and place it under the fish. This creates a faux fillet, which will make getting this side off in one pretty piece much, much easier.

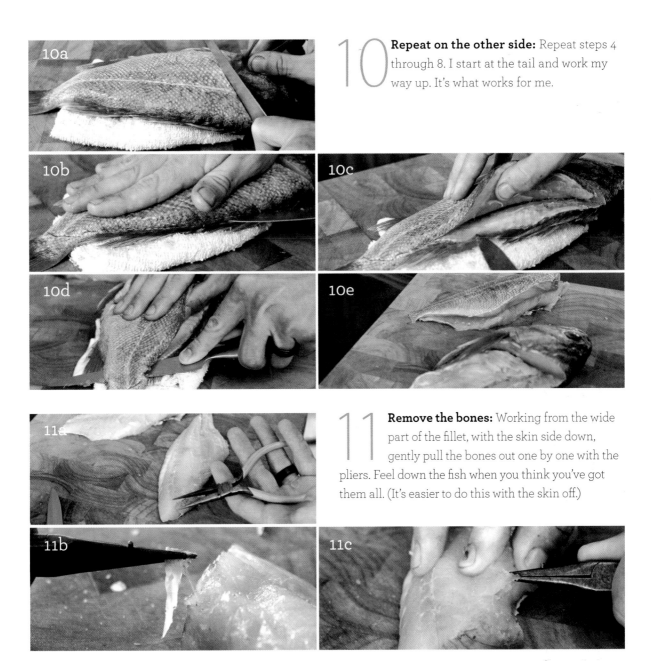

10 **Repeat on the other side:** Repeat steps 4 through 8. I start at the tail and work my way up. It's what works for me.

11 **Remove the bones:** Working from the wide part of the fillet, with the skin side down, gently pull the bones out one by one with the pliers. Feel down the fish when you think you've got them all. (It's easier to do this with the skin off.)

12 **Remove the skin:** If you are going to cook the fish without the skin, take it off by sliding the knife in between the skin and the meat starting at the tail, with the skin on the board. Let the knife point slightly down so that if you mess up you cut skin, not meat. It's more about getting ahold of the tail end and pulling it towards you while holding the knife still.

I have taken apart thousands of fish and this works for me, but others go about it in different ways and get a good result as well. Buy some cheap fish whole and give it a try. Fry up the mistakes with almond flour; toss with some sesame oil, a touch of fish sauce, and a handful of chopped chives; and serve with Baconnaise (page 256). Now that is one delicious learning experience.

Note that this is a method for filleting regular fish, not flat fish such as halibut or flounder.

FLAVORS OF SPRING

This season, more than any other, is about having a light hand in the kitchen. It's far too easy to overdo things at this time of year. You want to allow the ingredients to speak for themselves. The last thing you want to do is overpower them with too many flavorings and spices.

Intense, fresh, and clean flavors dominate with produce like ramps, asparagus, snap peas, artichokes, fiddleheads, and on and on. Simple and quick cooking methods let you retain and enhance the most flavor from every ingredient. Spring produce also pairs well with lighter proteins like poultry and fish, which lend themselves to similar methods of cooking. Whatever you do, keep it simple and try to get to a couple different farmers markets a week. There's just so much good stuff out there—you don't want to miss out.

SPRING

GARLIC SCAPES
ASPARAGUS **NETTLES** RHUBARB
SWEET
POTATOES CAULIFLOWER **SPINACH**
ARUGULA **WATERCRESS**
MUSHROOMS BOK CHOY
LIMES MUSTARD GREENS **PEAS**
ARTICHOKES
LEMONS
AVOCADOS
MORELS

ASPARAGUS **RADISH** CELERY
LETTUCE CARROTS CHARD SNAP PEAS/
TOMATOES GARLIC PEA PODS
AVOCADOS **COLLARD GREENS**
SUMMMER **LEEKS** **SORREL**
SQUASH **ONIONS**
KALE **PEAS** LEMONS

CARROTS
LETTUCE
MUSHROOMS
ASPARAGUS
PEA GREENS
ARUGULA

PARSLEY

CHARD
RADISH
RHUBARB
PARSNIP

GARLIC SCAPES
FAVA BEANS
SPINACH
MORELS

RAMPS
NETTLES
STINGING
NETTLES
PEA GREENS
PARSNIP RHUBARB
CHARD PARSLEY
ASPARAGUS
WILD MUSHROOMS
GARLIC SCAPES RADISH
FIDDLEHEADS
FAVA BEANS
MORELS

FENNEL
WILD
MUSHROOMS SUMMMER
SQUASH
CABBAGE NETTLES
MUSHROOMS RADISH
PEA GREENS
CARROTS BROCCOLI
TOMATOES SPINACH
CAULIFLOWER PEPPERS
FAVA BEANS TOMATILLOS
ASPARAGUS CHARD
MORELS
BEETS

BRINED AND ROASTED CHICKEN WITH CIDER PAN SAUCE

SERVES 4 · COOK TIME 1 HOUR, PLUS 12 TO 24 HOURS TO BRINE

INGREDIENTS

FOR THE BRINE (YIELD: 2 CUPS)

1 CUP WATER

1 TABLESPOON SALT

1 TABLESPOON HONEY (OPTIONAL)

1 TEASPOON BLACK PEPPERCORNS

1 BAY LEAF

1 CUP ICE

1 (2- TO 3-POUND) CHICKEN

2 TABLESPOONS DRIED THYME

1 TABLESPOON DRIED ROSEMARY

½ TABLESPOON CRACKED BLACK PEPPER

½ TABLESPOON SALT

½ CUP HARD CIDER (SEE NOTE)

½ CUP CHICKEN STOCK (PAGE 270)

1 TABLESPOON GHEE

* Note: I like Crispin Trappist cider for this sauce, but you could also use mead or wine, depending on the season and what you have on hand.

A quick note on brining in general: A chemical interaction between the salt solution and the meat cells injects the meat with your delicious brine, making it juicy and flavorful. What's more, the salt physically degenerates the protein—that is, it tenderizes it. Brining is magic, and it can be used on any poultry or pork cuts.

If you are unsure how much brine you will need, place the chicken in the pan you will be using to brine it and cover it with water. Then remove the chicken and measure the amount of water used. This is how much brine you will need to prepare. The recipe here makes 2 cups, so adjust the measurements as needed.

Bring the water to a boil in a large saucepan. Add the remaining brine ingredients and bring to a boil once more. Turn off the heat and add the ice to chill quickly.

Once the ice has melted, place the chicken in a roasting pan or other deep pan or pot and cover with the brine. Place in the refrigerator for at least 12 hours and up to 24 hours. Then remove the chicken from the brine, rinse it well, and pat it completely dry.

Preheat the oven to 450°F.

In a small bowl, mix together the thyme, rosemary, black pepper, and salt. Rub the mixture over chicken skin. Place the bird breast side up in a 9-by-13-inch roasting pan and roast for 50 minutes. Remove from the oven when the thigh meat is at 155°F or the juices run clear when a knife is inserted into the thigh meat.

Place the bird on a cutting board to rest and place the roasting pan on the stovetop over medium-high heat.

Pour the cider and stock into the pan and scrape the bottom with a wooden spatula or spoon. After about 3 minutes of rapid reduction, turn the heat off, add the ghee, and stir until melted and combined.

Let the sauce sit for a few minutes while you butcher the chicken (see page 21). Pour the sauce over the chicken if plating individually or serve it on the side if serving family style.

BLOOD ORANGE GLAZED PORK CHOPS

SERVES 4 · COOK TIME 45 MINUTES

Both boneless and bone-in pork chops will work with this dish, but bone-in will always make it tastier.

INGREDIENTS

ZEST OF 5 BLOOD ORANGES

1 TABLESPOON SALT

½ TABLESPOON FRESHLY GROUND BLACK PEPPER

4 PORK CHOPS, 1 INCH THICK

½ CUP CHICKEN STOCK (PAGE 270)

JUICE OF 5 BLOOD ORANGES

1 TABLESPOON GHEE OR COCONUT OIL

Preheat the oven to 375°F.

In a ramekin, combine the zest, salt, and pepper. Rub the mix into the chops and set aside to rest for 30 minutes.

While the chops are resting, simmer the stock and blood orange juice in a small saucepot over high heat for 20 minutes, or until reduced by half, then remove from heat and set aside. Be careful when reducing as the juice can boil over easily.

In a cast iron pan over medium-high heat, add the ghee. Once the pan is hot, sear the pork chops on one side until golden-brown, then flip over and cook for 2 minutes on the other side. Transfer the cast iron pan to the oven and cook for 8 to 12 minutes. Remove from the oven (careful, the cast iron pan will be very hot and heavy), place the chops on a cutting board, and let rest for 5 minutes. Serve with the glaze on the side or poured on top.

Reducing the stock and orange juice into a glaze is a painfully simple process, yet it can be difficult to get right. Just when you're sure it will never get thick, suddenly it does, and then just as quickly, it's gone too far and burns. Keep your eye on it towards the end of reduction; you'll get the hang of it after a couple times. If it burns, no big deal; just try again. And when it's done right, the reduction perfectly coats the back of a spoon, the meat, and your mouth.

CLASSIC BURGERS

SERVES 4 • COOK TIME 15 MINUTES

This recipe is the perfect base for any burgers you want to make. You can remove the shallots or the garlic or both, you can add roasted poblano peppers, or capers, or olives, or bacon, or sautéed and chopped mushrooms—you get the idea. Burgers are easy to customize and a great way to use whatever's in season.

Although it's not necessary, I like to let the burgers sit out for about 30 minutes before cooking. It helps the meat to cook faster and more evenly.

INGREDIENTS

1 SHALLOT, FINELY DICED

2 TABLESPOONS OLIVE OIL, DIVIDED

2 CLOVES GARLIC, MINCED

2 POUNDS GRASS-FED GROUND BEEF

1 TABLESPOON SALT

½ TABLESPOON CRACKED BLACK PEPPER

In a medium sauté pan over medium-high heat, sauté the shallot in 1 tablespoon of the olive oil until they are translucent, about 4 minutes. Add the garlic and cook through. Transfer the shallot and garlic mixture to a plate and throw it in the fridge to cool down quickly.

In a large bowl, combine the cooled shallot and garlic, ground beef, salt, pepper, and the remaining tablespoon of olive oil. Mix thoroughly with your hands. Your hands are pretty much the best tool you'll ever find in the kitchen. Wash them often and don't be afraid to use 'em.

Form the meat mixture into four ½-inch-thick patties. Use your thumb to make a small indentation in one side of the patty—that way, when the heat hits the beef and makes it contract, it stays in patty form instead of turning into a ball.

Heat a cast iron pan over medium-high heat. Ideally your pan is very well seasoned, but if not, add a tablespoon of avocado oil to the pan. When the pan is good and hot, add the patties starting at 12 o'clock and moving clockwise. If your pan can't hold all four, cook two at a time. Cook for 4 minutes, or until the patties have a good brown crust, and flip them over. Cook on the other side for 3 to 4 minutes for a medium-rare burger. If you want them cooked further, you can finish them in a 400°F oven for 5 minutes or turn down the heat so they don't burn and cook them longer in the pan.

Let the burgers rest for 2 to 3 minutes before serving. Enjoy them on top of a salad, with a lettuce wrap, with some Brussels sprouts, avocado, and mushrooms, or with just about anything else.

PAN-SEARED DUCK BREAST

SERVES 4 • COOK TIME 15 TO 20 MINUTES, PLUS 24 HOURS TO BRINE

Make sure you have enough brine to cover the duck breasts completely. The recipe here makes 2 cups, so adjust the measurements as needed.

INGREDIENTS

FOR THE BRINE (YIELD: 2 CUPS)

1 CUP WATER

1 TABLESPOON SALT

1 TABLESPOON HONEY (OPTIONAL)

1 TEASPOON BLACK PEPPERCORNS

1 BAY LEAF

1 CUP ICE

4 DUCK BREASTS (1½ POUNDS TOTAL)

Bring the water to a boil in a large saucepan. Add the remaining brine ingredients and bring to a boil once more. Turn off the heat and add the ice to chill quickly.

Once the ice has melted, place the duck breasts in a roasting pan and cover with the brine. Place in the refrigerator for at least 12 hours and up to 24 hours. Then remove the duck breasts from the brine, rinse well, and pat completely dry.

Preheat the oven to 375°F.

Heat a large sauté pan (at least 12 by 12 inches) or two medium sauté pans over medium heat. Do not add oil to the pan.

Once pan is hot, add the duck breasts skin side down and cook for 8 to 10 minutes. Avoid moving the duck to get a dark sear, which is key. Flip and sear for 3 minutes, then, again without moving the duck, pour off the excess fat. Place the pan in the oven and finish for 3 to 4 minutes.

The duck can be served as-is or sliced into ¼-inch-wide strips and used in the Panang Duck Curry on page 42.

PANANG DUCK CURRY

SERVES 4 TO 6 · COOK TIME 40 MINUTES, PLUS TIME TO BRINE AND COOK THE DUCK BREAST

INGREDIENTS

1 (13½-OUNCE) CAN COCONUT MILK

1 STALK LEMONGRASS, SMASHED WITH BACK OF LARGE CHEF'S KNIFE AND TOP TWO-THIRDS REMOVED

1 TABLESPOON PEELED AND FINELY GRATED FRESH GINGER

3 TABLESPOONS OLIVE OIL

1 LARGE YELLOW ONION (1 POUND), CUT INTO MEDIUM DICE

1 LARGE CARROT (10 OUNCES), SLICED

1 TEASPOON SALT

2 MEDIUM RED, YELLOW, OR ORANGE BELL PEPPERS (ABOUT 1 SCANT POUND), CUT INTO MEDIUM DICE

2 HEADS BABY BOK CHOY (12 OUNCES TOTAL), CUT INTO STRIPS 1 INCH WIDE

4 OUNCES MUSHROOMS, CUT INTO SLICES ¼ INCH THICK

½ POUND SUGAR SNAP PEAS

1 RECIPE PAN-SEARED DUCK BREAST (PAGE 40), SLICED INTO STRIPS 1 INCH WIDE

2 TABLESPOON PANANG OR RED CURRY PASTE

2 TABLESPOONS THAI BASIL LEAVES, TORN

2 TABLESPOONS MINT LEAVES, PICKED AND TORN AT THE LAST MINUTE

MANGO CAULIFLOWER STICKY RICE (PAGE 50), FOR SERVING

This dish is about highlighting super fresh spring vegetables and wrapping them in tasty flavors that complement them without being overpowering. By far the star is the sugar snap peas. They always remind me of walking through my neighbor's garden when I was little, picking the first to appear in early spring and eating them fresh off the vine. So clean and sweet, so spring.

In a medium sauté pan, bring the coconut milk and lemongrass stalk to a slow simmer over very low heat. Continue to cook this at a low simmer as you prepare the remaining elements of the dish. After the coconut mixture has been simmering for 15 minutes, add the ginger and simmer for another 10 to 15 minutes.

Heat a wok or a very large sauté pan over medium-high heat, then add the oil. Add the onion and sauté for 3 minutes. Add the carrot and salt and sauté for another 3 minutes. Add the bell peppers, bok choy, mushrooms, and sugar snap peas and sauté for 3 to 4 minutes. The vegetables should be tender but still have a very light crunch.

Strain the coconut milk mixture and discard the stalk of lemongrass and the pulp from the ginger. Add the duck and strained coconut milk to the pan with the vegetables. Stir well and cook just long enough to heat the duck through. Fold in the curry paste, then remove from the heat, add the Thai basil and mint, and gently stir. Serve with Mango Cauliflower Sticky Rice (page 50).

PORK LOIN WRAPPED IN BACON

SERVES 4 · COOK TIME 30 MINUTES

Blanching bacon is somewhat counter-intuitive, but it renders some of the fat, which helps the bacon crisp up and keeps it from shriveling, so it will wrap the tenderloin better. Plus, any time you blanch bacon, you create bacon stock, the perfect base for potato and leek soup.

INGREDIENTS

6 OUNCES BACON, THINLY SLICED

1½ POUNDS PORK TENDERLOIN, CUT INTO 5-OUNCE PIECES ABOUT 2 INCHES THICK

SALT

Preheat the oven to 400°F.

Blanch the bacon for 3 minutes and lay it on a plate lined with paper towels.

Lightly sprinkle the pieces of tenderloin with salt and wrap them in the bacon.

Place the wrapped tenderloin in a cold, thick-bottomed, oven-safe sauté pan over medium-high heat. Start with the side with the bacon ends on the bottom of the pan, so that it cooks first and the bacon ends seal closed. Cook for roughly 7 to 8 minutes on this side. Then rotate the tenderloin along its edge, cooking to a golden-brown all the way around. You should spend roughly 3 to 4 minutes on every side once the pan is nice and hot.

Transfer the pork loin to a roast rack, again with the bacon ends on the bottom, letting gravity help keep it together. Roast for approximately 9 minutes. If, like me, you prefer your pork cooked medium, around 140°F and with a medium-pink center, cook it for slightly less time—around 6 minutes is perfect.

Remove the pork from the oven and let it rest on a cutting board for 4 to 6 minutes. If you put a few paper towels down underneath the loin before cutting it, the runoff juices will be absorbed, saving you a mess on the board and, more importantly, on your pretty plate. Cut into ½-inch-thick slices, using a sharp slicing or chef's knife.

Pictured here with with Romanesco and Sweet Potatoes (page 168).

BATTERED FISH TACOS

SERVES 2 TO 3 · COOK TIME 6 MINUTES, PLUS 1 HOUR TO MAKE THE SPICY CABBAGE SLAW

I love frying fish, and how people handle themselves on a fry station is a sign of how well they cook. Do they work clean, without getting egg and batter everywhere? Do they get the fish just right, not burning or overcooking it? It's worth the time and practice to get good at it.

To make this meal come together more quickly, make the slaw the day before.

INGREDIENTS

1 POUND HALIBUT OR OTHER WHITE FISH FILLETS, SUCH AS GROUPER, COD, OR POLLOCK, CUT INTO "FINGERS" A LITTLE THICKER THAN YOUR THUMB AND A BIT LONGER THAN YOUR INDEX FINGER (SEE NOTES)

1 CUP OLIVE OIL PLUS MORE AS NEEDED (SEE NOTES)

FOR THE EGG WASH

1 LARGE EGG

3 TABLESPOONS WATER

1 TEASPOON SALT

FOR THE ALMOND FLOUR COATING

2 CUPS FINE ALMOND FLOUR

1 TEASPOON SALT

1 TEASPOON FRESHLY GROUND BLACK PEPPER

SEVERAL BUTTER LETTUCE LEAVES, FOR SERVING

SEVERAL LIME WEDGES, FOR SERVING

SPICY CABBAGE SLAW (PAGE 52), FOR SERVING

If you don't have leftover cabbage slaw, make that first, since it needs to marinate for at least 50 minutes.

Pat the fish completely dry with paper towels.

Pour the olive oil into a heavy sauté pan until it comes approximately ½ inch up the sides of the pan. (You want an amount that will reach halfway up the sides of the fish.) Slowly heat the oil over medium heat.

While the oil is heating, prepare the wash and dry coating: In a shallow bowl, whisk together the ingredients for the egg wash. In another shallow bowl, whisk together the ingredients for the almond flour coating.

Next, set up your assembly line: First comes your well-dried fish. Next is the egg wash, then the almond flour coating, followed by the pan with hot oil, and finally a plate or sheet pan lined with a paper towel, for the fried fish.

Always use equal parts egg and liquid in washes. Although a good rule of thumb is that a large egg is about 3 tablespoons in volume, all eggs vary slightly, so adjust the amount of liquid as needed.

Notes: Tilapia work well here, but the environmental impact of some tilapia farms ranges from iffy to downright bad. If you can find a responsible source, however, it's a good substitute.

In place of olive oil you can use coconut oil or duck fat. I like to use olive oil when frying fish because it smokes when the oil is getting too hot. It's best to cook fish at a temperature that isn't too hot, so this visual cue comes in handy.

When the oil reaches 300°F, it's ready. If you do not have a deep-fat thermometer, check if the oil has a shimmer and a wave to it; if it does, it's ready to use. If it begins to smoke, it's too hot. You can test the heat by dropping a pinch of almond flour in it; if it sizzles, it is hot enough.

It is best to work in batches of two or three fish pieces. Any more than this and things tend to get messy; plus, it lets you get back to the first piece of fish in the pan in time to flip it. It is important to have one wet hand and one dry hand when completing the batter process. To keep the process tidy, I typically wash my hands between batches.

Using your wet hand, place the fish into the egg wash, then, with the same hand, drop the fish into the flour.

Use your dry hand to turn and coat the fish in the flour mixture and then carefully place it in the oil.

In 3 minutes the flour coating will start to turn golden-brown. Flip the fish and start coating the next round. Once flipped, the fish should cook another 2 to 3 minutes. It will turn one shade darker once you remove it from the oil, so pull it from the oil before you think it is done. I'm serious about this: when you are sure in every fiber of your being that it needs more time, that's when it's time to take it out. Set the fish on the paper towel–lined plate or sheet pan to drain.

Serve in a butter lettuce leaf, topped with cabbage slaw and a wedge of lime.

FRIED CAULIFLOWER RICE

SERVES 4 • COOK TIME 20 MINUTES

I like to add pork to this dish, but there are limitless variations for this recipe. You can add any protein your little heart desires: chicken, shrimp, steak, boar, camel, snake, turtle, whatever. You can also replace the vegetables with whatever you find at the market.

INGREDIENTS

1 HEAD CAULIFLOWER

1 TABLESPOON COCONUT OIL

1 POUND FRESH SNAP PEAS, SHUCKED

1 ANAHEIM CHILE, SEEDED AND FINELY DICED

1 JALAPEÑO PEPPER, SEEDED AND FINELY DICED (OPTIONAL)

2 MEDIUM CARROTS, SLICED (ABOUT 1 CUP)

2 PINCHES OF SALT, DIVIDED, PLUS MORE TO TASTE

½ CUP CHICKEN STOCK (PAGE 270), DIVIDED

½ CUP SLICED SCALLION OR LEEK

1 TABLESPOON COCONUT AMINOS

2 TABLESPOONS CHOPPED FRESH MINT

Remove the stem and leaves from the cauliflower and discard. Using a paring knife, cut the cauliflower into medium florets and remove any remaining stems.

Pulse the cauliflower florets in a food processor for 5 to 10 seconds and repeat until the cauliflower is the size of cooked grains of rice. (Using the pulse button instead of continuously processing helps keep the cauliflower from turning to mush or processing unevenly.)

In a large sauté pan over medium heat, melt the coconut oil and then add the peas, Anaheim chile, jalapeño, carrots, and a pinch of salt and stir together. Sauté for 4 to 6 minutes, then add ¼ cup of the chicken stock. This will soften the carrots and peas as well as deglaze your pan for its delicious fond.

Once the stock has cooked down, after about 3 to 4 minutes, add the scallions and half of the cauliflower rice. (You can save the rest for another rice recipe, or double the other ingredients for this recipe and make a huge batch you can eat all week.) Add another pinch of salt and continue to sauté for 4 to 6 minutes. Once the cauliflower rice has been mixed with the other ingredients, avoid stirring too much so that it can get nice and brown.

Add the remaining ¼ cup of chicken stock to deglaze the pan. Scrape the pan with your spatula to get all the goodness off the bottom. Transfer the cauliflower rice mixture to a serving dish, season with the coconut aminos, and mix in the mint. Season with salt to taste.

MANGO CAULIFLOWER STICKY RICE

SERVES 6 • COOK TIME 15 MINUTES

INGREDIENTS

1 MEDIUM HEAD CAULIFLOWER

1 RIPE MANGO

1½ CUPS CHICKEN STOCK (PAGE 270) OR VEGETABLE STOCK, OR 1 CUP CHICKEN OR VEGETABLE STOCK AND ½ CUP COCONUT MILK, PLUS MORE STOCK AS NEEDED

Remove the stem and leaves from the cauliflower and discard. Using a paring knife, cut the cauliflower into medium florets and remove any remaining stems.

Pulse the cauliflower florets in a food processor for 5 to 10 seconds and repeat until the cauliflower is the size of cooked grains of rice. (Using the pulse button instead of continuously processing helps keep the cauliflower from turning to mush or processing unevenly.)

Peel and finely chop the mango. Use caution when cutting around the seed of a mango. It is easy to lose where the seed is and cut yourself or, worse, leave a lot of mango on the seed. Take your time and get it all off. There's no need to make it pretty; your focus is getting all the mango you can.

Place the cauliflower, mango, and stock in a medium saucepan and bring to a boil over medium-high heat. Reduce the heat to medium-low and continue to simmer, uncovered, for 10 minutes. The liquid will reduce and the cauliflower will become tender.

If the liquid has not evaporated, turn the heat up until it's at a rolling boil and cook until liquid is gone. If the liquid is gone but the cauliflower is not tender, add an additional ¼ cup of stock and continue to cook.

SPICY CABBAGE SLAW

SERVES 6 · COOK TIME 1 HOUR TO MARINATE

This recipe goes beautifully with Battered Fish Tacos (page 46), and it's also great on burgers or as a salad with greens. My wife has even been known to eat it straight out of the bowl. It gets better the longer it marinates, and it will last for one week in the fridge.

In a medium bowl, mix together the sesame oil, fish sauce, lime zest, lime juice, cilantro, vinegar, and Sriracha sauce. Allow to sit for at least 20 to 30 minutes, then add the cabbage, carrot, and chives and toss it all together. Let sit for 30 minutes before serving.

INGREDIENTS

3 TABLESPOONS TOASTED SESAME OIL

2 TEASPOONS FISH SAUCE, SUCH AS RED BOAT FISH SAUCE

ZEST OF ½ LIME

JUICE OF 1 LIME

1 TABLESPOON CHOPPED FRESH CILANTRO

1 TABLESPOON APPLE CIDER VINEGAR

2 TEASPOONS SRIRACHA SAUCE

½ HEAD RED CABBAGE (ABOUT ½ POUND), CORED AND THINLY SLICED (ABOUT 3 CUPS)

1 LARGE CARROT, JULIENNED (ABOUT 1 CUP)

1 TABLESPOON CHOPPED FRESH CHIVES

ROASTED CARROT PUREE

YIELD 1 CUP • COOK TIME 25 MINUTES

INGREDIENTS

1 BUNCH BABY CARROTS, ROUGHLY CHOPPED (KEEP THE GREENS FOR CARROT PISTOU, PAGE 56)

1 SHALLOT, HALVED

1 TABLESPOON OLIVE OIL

½ TEASPOON SALT

½ TEASPOON FRESHLY GROUND BLACK PEPPER

¼ CUP CHICKEN STOCK (PAGE 270) OR VEGETABLE STOCK, ROOM TEMPERATURE

2 TEASPOONS BACON FAT OR GHEE, CHILLED

Preheat the oven to 400°F.

Spread the carrots evenly on a sheet pan and mix with the shallot, olive oil, salt, and pepper. Roast for 25 minutes, or until the corners of the carrots are a light golden-brown.

Place the roasted carrots and shallot in a blender. Add the stock, which needs to be at room temperature, and blend until smooth. With the blender on, add the chilled bacon fat to emulsify the mixture.

CARROT PISTOU

YIELD 2 CUPS

INGREDIENTS

TOPS FROM ONE BUNCH BABY CARROTS (ABOUT ½ CUP)

½ GALA APPLE, ROUGHLY CHOPPED

1 TABLESPOON LEMON JUICE

1 TEASPOON LEMON ZEST

¼ TEASPOON SALT

¼ CUP OLIVE OIL

Blanch the carrot greens for 15 seconds, dip in an ice bath, and pat dry.

In a blender or food processor, combine the carrot greens, apple, lemon juice, zest, salt, and olive oil. Process to a lightly chunky texture; taste and add more salt, lemon juice, or zest if needed. Since the amount of carrot greens will always vary, you'll want to season to taste.

GRILLED ARTICHOKE AND SHIITAKE MUSHROOM SALAD WITH ROASTED GARLIC

SERVES 2 • COOK TIME 35 MINUTES

INGREDIENTS

8 TO 12 CLOVES GARLIC (SEE NOTE)

1 TEASPOON PLUS 1 TABLESPOON AVOCADO OIL, DIVIDED

2 MEDIUM ARTICHOKES

8 OUNCES SHIITAKE MUSHROOMS

¼ TEASPOON SALT

FOR THE DRESSING

1 TABLESPOON OLIVE OIL

1 TEASPOON APPLE CIDER VINEGAR OR LEMON JUICE

¼ TEASPOON LEMON ZEST

1 TABLESPOON CHOPPED FRESH PARSLEY

¼ TEASPOON FRESHLY GROUND BLACK PEPPER

¼ TEASPOON SALT

Note: Pre-peeled garlic cloves may be used.

ROAST THE GARLIC

Preheat the oven to 325°F. Lightly coat the garlic cloves with 1 teaspoon of the avocado oil and spread on a sheet pan. Bake for 20 minutes, stirring halfway through the cooking process, until the cloves are golden but still slightly firm.

PREP AND GRILL THE ARTICHOKES

Preheat the grill to high heat. Using a sharp knife, remove the hearts from the artichokes: First, cut off the top inch of the artichoke. Turn the artichoke upside down so the stem is facing up. Cut down the sides to remove all the leaves. Once the leaves have been removed, cut off more of the top to expose the choke. The choke is the fuzzy part, and it is not edible. Use a spoon or melon baller to scoop out all the choke. Make sure to remove all the fuzzy hairs. Cut off all but 1 inch of the stem. Continue to clean up the side by removing the base of the leaves; be careful because the heart is very delicate. You may want to use a paring knife for the final trimming.

To prevent sticking, oil the grill by quickly rubbing the grates with an old, clean kitchen towel dabbed in a small amount of oil. Cut the artichoke in half from top to bottom. Once the grill is hot, make hash marks on the flat side of the artichoke: Place the artichoke flat side down on the very hot grill for 1 minute, turn 90 degrees, and cook for 1 more minute. Flip over and repeat, cooking for a total of approximately 4 minutes. Be careful not overcook or the artichoke will get chewy. When the artichokes are cool enough to handle, cut them into bite-sized pieces.

PREP AND GRILL THE SHIITAKES

Remove and discard the mushroom stems. (Shiitake mushroom stems are useless; they are the only mushroom whose stem you have to discard.)

Lightly coat the shiitakes with the remaining 1 tablespoon of avocado oil and the salt. Grill them the same way you did the artichoke hearts: Place them cap side down, grill 1 to 2 minutes, turn 90 degrees, and grill 1 to 2 minutes more. Flip over and repeat, cooking for a total of 4 to 8 minutes. (The exact time will depend on the temperature of the grill.) You want to get a deep color with the grill marks, but you don't want to overcook the mushrooms, as they will start to turn slimy. Cut the grilled mushroom caps into halves or quarters depending on the size of the caps.

In a small bowl, combine the dressing ingredients. In a separate large serving bowl, place the garlic cloves, artichokes, and shiitake mushrooms. Add the dressing and toss to evenly coat. Taste and add an extra pinch of salt if needed.

ARUGULA, STRAWBERRY, AND RADISH SALAD WITH BALSAMIC VINAIGRETTE

SERVES 4

I always serve my salads tossed with dressing. It looks better and evens out the dressing and seasoning. It's very important for every bite of salad to have the clean and bitter flavor of the greens, the acid, salt, and other spices. This is only guaranteed when you mix the salad together before serving.

INGREDIENTS

1 CUP SLICED RADISH (ANY KIND AS LONG AS IT'S FRESH)

1½ CUPS SLICED SPRING STRAWBERRIES

1 SHALLOT, THINLY SLICED

4 CUPS FRESH ARUGULA

½ CUP BALSAMIC VINAIGRETTE (PAGE 264)

In a large bowl, toss together the radish, strawberries, shallot, and arugula. Drizzle the vinaigrette on top and toss.

SHAVED ASPARAGUS AND BEET SALAD

SERVES 4

This salad gets very tender and flavorful as it marinates. I recommend making it at least 30 to 90 minutes before serving.

INGREDIENTS

½ BUNCH ASPARAGUS (8 OUNCES; SEE NOTE)

1 SMALL YELLOW ONION

1 SMALL GOLDEN BEET (6 TO 8 OUNCES)

1 SMALL BUNCH KALE

3 TABLESPOONS OLIVE OIL

2 TABLESPOONS APPLE CIDER VINEGAR

1 TEASPOON SALT

½ TEASPOON FRESHLY GROUND BLACK PEPPER

* Note: When purchasing asparagus, always look for thin stalks. As they grow and get larger, they become more fibrous and tough.

Remove the fibrous bottoms of the asparagus by gently bending the bottom of each spear. The bottom third or so should easily break off. Slice the asparagus and the onion thinly on a mandoline or by hand, making sure to slice the asparagus at an angle.

Peel the beet and slice thinly on the mandoline or by hand. Once the beet is sliced, immediately place it in cold water to keep it from turning brown.

Stem and julienne the kale (you should have 3 to 4 cups).

Mix all the vegetables in a serving bowl and toss with the olive oil, vinegar, salt, and pepper. Let marinate for at least 30 minutes before serving. It will keep for 1 week in the fridge.

BACON AND SHAVED BRUSSELS SPROUTS SALAD

SERVES 4 AS A SIDE • COOK TIME 15 MINUTES

Brussels sprouts grow in the spring in the Baja region of San Diego and are a great addition to your spring vegetable options where available.

INGREDIENTS

¾ POUND BRUSSELS SPROUTS

½ CUP RAW PECANS

4 OUNCES BACON, CUT INTO STRIPS 1 INCH BY ¼ INCH

¼ TEASPOON SALT

⅓ CUP CHICKEN STOCK (PAGE 270) OR VEGETABLE STOCK

1 TEASPOON BALSAMIC VINEGAR, TO FINISH

Preheat the oven to 350°F. Bring a pot of water to a boil.

Blanch the Brussels sprouts in the boiling water for 2 minutes. Using a slotted spoon, remove them from the water and immediately place them in an ice water bath or rinse under cold running water for 3 to 4 minutes.

Slice the bottoms off of the Brussels sprouts, cutting the stem rather high so the larger outer leaves fall off easily. Slip off the outer leaves and place them in a bowl, then thinly slice the Brussels sprouts on a mandoline or by hand. Add the shaved Brussels sprouts to the bowl with the leaves.

Place the pecans on a sheet pan and roast for 10 minutes, or until golden-brown. Roughly chop the pecans or crumble them by hand.

Heat a medium sauté pan over medium heat and add the bacon. Cook for approximately 8 to 10 minutes to render the fat and lightly brown the bacon.

Keeping all the rendered fat in the pan, carefully add the Brussels sprouts and continue to cook on high heat for approximately 5 minutes. Do not stir often; you want a nice brown color on the Brussels sprouts. Stir in the roasted pecans and salt. Add the stock, then scrape the bottom of pan with a wooden spoon and remove from heat.

Drizzle on the balsamic vinegar and serve. This dish is best served warm and eaten right away.

CARROT LEMONGRASS SOUP

SERVES 4 • YIELD 1 QUART • COOK TIME 50 MINUTES

INGREDIENTS

3 TABLESPOONS GHEE

1 SMALL ONION, FINELY DICED (ABOUT 1 CUP)

1 POUND CARROTS, PEELED AND ROUGHLY CHOPPED

½ TABLESPOON SALT, DIVIDED

4 CUPS VEGETABLE OR CHICKEN STOCK (PAGE 270)

1 STALK LEMONGRASS, TOP HALF CUT OFF AND BOTTOM HALF WHACKED WITH THE BACK OF A BIG METAL SPOON

½ TEASPOON WHITE PEPPER

½ TEASPOON TURMERIC

In a large saucepot, add the ghee over medium-high heat. When the ghee is hot, about 4 minutes, add the onion, carrots, and ¼ tablespoon of the salt. Let the onion and carrots roast in the pan, stirring occasionally, for 12 to 15 minutes, or until the bottom of the pan and the vegetables are golden-brown. Add the stock, deglazing and scraping the brown fond from the bottom. Add the lemongrass, white pepper, and turmeric and turn the heat down to medium-low.

Simmer for 25 to 30 minutes, or until the carrots are fork-tender. Remove the lemongrass stalk, transfer the soup in batches to a blender or food processor, and puree.

Add the remaining ¼ tablespoon of salt, plus more to taste, and serve. The soup will keep in the fridge for 10 days and in the freezer for 6 months.

Make sure you puree the soup in small batches: if you add a ton of hot soup to a blender and turn it on, it will explode through the top and, if it doesn't burn you, make a horrible mess. Don't fill the blender or processor more than a third of the way up for each batch.

FLAVORS OF SUMMER

Summer always reminds me of the picnics my family used to host for all our friends and family, with volleyball, bocce ball, macaroni salad, Aunt Suzie's seven-layer taco dip, and of course barbecue. This time of year, the more time that can be spent around a grill and a smoker, the better.

Much like spring, summer is about using simple cooking methods to highlight the abundance of fresh produce and the flavors that compose the season's bounty.

SUMMER

PLUMS AND PLUOTS ZUCCHINI GREEN ONIONS
TOMATOES RADISH EGGPLANT
MUSHROOMS CUCUMBERS
CHILES GREEN BEANS BASIL
PARSNIPS SUMMER PEPPERS
CHARD SQUASH AVOCADOS
BROCCOLI
PEAS

GARLIC PUMPKINS WINTER CHILES
ONIONS PEPPERS SQUASH
SUMMER GREEN BEANS CUCUMBERS
SQUASH TOMATOES EGGPLANT
LEEKS
SHELLING BEANS
TOMATILLOS
FIGS

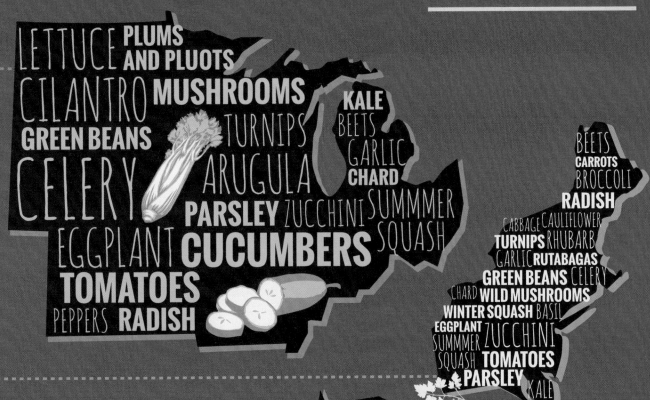

LETTUCE PLUMS AND PLUOTS
CILANTRO MUSHROOMS
GREEN BEANS TURNIPS KALE
BEETS
CELERY ARUGULA GARLIC
CHARD
PARSLEY ZUCCHINI SUMMMER
SQUASH
EGGPLANT CUCUMBERS
TOMATOES
PEPPERS RADISH

BEETS
CARROTS
BROCCOLI
RADISH
CABBAGE CAULIFLOWER
TURNIPS RHUBARB
GARLIC RUTABAGAS
GREEN BEANS CELERY
CHARD WILD MUSHROOMS
WINTER SQUASH BASIL
EGGPLANT ZUCCHINI
SUMMER
SQUASH TOMATOES
PARSLEY
KALE

BLUEBERRIES
ZUCCHINI BLOSSOMS
MUSHROOMS SHALLOTS
BELL PEPPERS PEPPERS
BEETS
OKRA
TOMATOES SWEET POTATOES
CARROTS
RADISH COLLARD GREENS RADICCHIO
CUCUMBERS SUMMMER SQUASH
EGGPLANT SPINACH RHUBARB
WILD CAULIFLOWER ONIONS POTATOES
MUSHROOMS
CABBAGE
WINTER
SQUASH
BASIL

CHERRY BRAISED LAMB SHOULDER

SERVES 4 TO 5 · COOK TIME 2½ HOURS

I like to serve this dish with a dill cauliflower rice. It's easy to make: cook Fried Cauliflower Rice (page 48) without the vegetables, sauté the rice with 1 cup chopped yellow onion, and fold in 3 tablespoons chopped fresh dill.

INGREDIENTS

2 POUNDS LAMB SHOULDER

2 TABLESPOONS OLIVE OIL

1 LARGE ONION, THINLY SLICED (ABOUT 2 CUPS)

4 CUPS BEEF STOCK (PAGE 274), CHICKEN STOCK (PAGE 270), OR WATER

1 POUND CHERRIES, PITTED (FRESH IS BEST, BUT FROZEN WILL DO), DIVIDED

1½ TABLESPOONS SALT

1 TABLESPOON FRESHLY GROUND BLACK PEPPER

4 TABLESPOONS CHOPPED FRESH DILL

½ CUP PINE NUTS

Preheat the oven to 350°F.

Trim the lamb of as much silver skin as possible. Get rid of any excess fat, but don't worry about getting it all. Cut into ½-inch cubes roughly and set aside.

Heat the olive oil in a braising pan over medium-high heat. Once the oil is warmed through, add the onion and cook till translucent, about 3 minutes. Turn the heat as high as possible and push the onion to the outside of the pan. Add the lamb and don't touch it. Let it get nice and brown on one side, about 6 to 8 minutes, then stir once. Right before it gets to the point of burning, another 6 to 8 minutes, add the stock. Add ½ pound of the pitted cherries and the salt and pepper, stir, and cover the pan.

Transfer the pan to the oven and braise for 2 hours, or until the meat is fork-tender. Fold in the remaining ½ pound of cherries, the dill, and the pine nuts. Serve over dill cauliflower rice.

If you are working with fresh cherries, the easiest way to pit them is to put them on a sheet pan and smash them with the bottom of a sauté pan. You can't hurt them, so go after them. Then go through them carefully and separate the cleaned cherries into a bowl. Double-check them to be sure—trust me.

BURGERS WITH AVOCADO SALSA

SERVES 4 · COOK TIME 15 MINUTES

While this avocado salsa is similar to guacamole, I prefer to call it a salsa because it keeps the shape of the cut avocados—they aren't mashed into a paste, à la guacamole.

INGREDIENTS

2 POUNDS GROUND GRASS-FED BEEF

2 TABLESPOONS OLIVE OIL

1 TABLESPOON MINCED GARLIC

1 TABLESPOON SALT

1 TABLESPOON FRESHLY GROUND BLACK PEPPER

FOR THE SALSA

2 TO 3 RIPE HASS AVOCADOS

JUICE OF ½ LIME

ZEST OF ½ LIME

1 SMALL ROMA TOMATO, SEEDED AND DICED (ABOUT ½ CUP)

1 SMALL MANGO, PEELED AND DICED (ABOUT 1 CUP)

1 CLOVE GARLIC, MINCED (ABOUT 1 TABLESPOON)

1 SMALL SHALLOT, MINCED (ABOUT 3 TABLESPOONS)

3 TABLESPOONS CHOPPED CILANTRO

1 JALAPEÑO PEPPER, SEEDED AND FINELY DICED

1 TEASPOON SALT, PLUS MORE TO TASTE

1 TEASPOON PEPPER

½ TEASPOON GROUND CUMIN

½ TEASPOON CHILI POWDER

GRILL THE BURGERS

Preheat your grill. If you have a gas grill, set it on high; if you have a charcoal grill, use a chimney or propane starter.

In a large bowl, mix all the ingredients for the burgers with your hands. Form the mixture into four patties about 5 inches in diameter and ¾ inch thick. Place the burgers on a sheet pan, cover with plastic wrap, and let sit at room temperature for about 20 minutes. This will let the salt do some work on the meat and raise the temperature of the meat so it cooks evenly on the grill.

Place the burgers on the grill, beginning at 12 o'clock and working clockwise around the grill. Let the burgers grill for 3 to 4 minutes. Starting with the burger at 12 o'clock, turn each burger 90 degrees and cook for 1 to 2 minutes to get the perfect diamond-shaped char. Flip the burgers and cook for 2 to 3 minutes, then turn each burger 90 degrees and cook for 1 to 2 minutes.

MAKE THE SALSA

Halve the avocados and remove the pits. Without going through the peel, make diagonal slices ¼ inch wide across the avocado, then turn it 90 degrees and repeat to create ¼-inch cubes. Scoop out the avocado pieces into a bowl and immediately squeeze the lime juice over them so they don't start to brown. Zest the other half of the lime onto the avocado.

Add the tomato, mango, garlic, shallot, cilantro, jalapeño, salt, pepper, ground cumin, and chili powder. Fold the mixture together, keeping the shape of the avocado as intact as possible. Add more salt if necessary.

While the salsa can be eaten right away, it's great after 3 to 6 hours in the fridge, and it will keep in the fridge for 3 to 5 days.

Plate the burgers after they have rested for about 5 minutes, then top with a few tablespoons of salsa per burger.

GROUND ELK PATTIES WITH SPINACH AND SWEET POTATO

SERVES 4 · COOK TIME 40 MINUTES

INGREDIENTS

FOR THE ELK PATTIES

2 POUNDS GROUND ELK OR OTHER GROUND GAME, SUCH AS VENISON OR BOAR

1 SMALL ONION, DICED (ABOUT 1 CUP)

2 CLOVES GARLIC, MINCED (ABOUT 1 TABLESPOON)

1 TABLESPOON SALT

1 TABLESPOON FRESHLY GROUND BLACK PEPPER

1 TEASPOON PAPRIKA

1 TEASPOON TURMERIC

1 TEASPOON GROUND CORIANDER

2 TABLESPOONS OLIVE OIL

2 TABLESPOONS GHEE

1½ POUNDS SWEET POTATOES, CUT INTO MEDIUM DICE (ABOUT 4 CUPS)

1 TEASPOON SALT, DIVIDED

1 CUP CHICKEN STOCK (PAGE 270), DIVIDED

1 POUND SPINACH

1 TEASPOON FRESHLY GROUND BLACK PEPPER

Preheat the oven to 375°F.

In a large bowl, mix together all the ingredients for the elk patties using your hands. Form the mixture into little 2-ounce oblong meatballs, about 3 inches long. This should give you about 15 to 17 total. Place about 2 inches apart on an ungreased sheet pan and cook in the oven for 12 to 15 minutes, or until the internal temp reaches 145°F.

While the elk cooks, start the sweet potatoes and spinach: Add the ghee to a large cast iron pan over medium-high heat. Let the pan heat for 4 to 5 minutes, then add the sweet potatoes and ½ teaspoon of the salt. Let the potatoes roast for 6 to 8 minutes, stir, then continue cooking for another 6 to 8 minutes.

Deglaze the pan with ½ cup of the stock. Reduce the stock for 4 to 5 minutes, then let the potatoes roast again for 6 minutes. Stir and let cook for another 6 minutes, then add the spinach and the remaining ½ cup of stock. Let steam for 2 to 3 minutes, then stir to incorporate the spinach. Add the remaining ½ teaspoon of salt and the pepper.

Serve the elk over the sweet potatoes and spinach.

MEATBALLS WITH ZUCCHINI NOODLES AND PEACH BASIL SALSA

SERVES 4 • COOK TIME 30 MINUTES, PLUS 2 HOURS TO MAKE THE SALSA

INGREDIENTS

1 POUND GROUND PORK

1 POUND GROUND LAMB

1 TABLESPOON PLUS 1 TEASPOON SALT, DIVIDED

½ TABLESPOON FRESHLY GROUND BLACK PEPPER

1 TEASPOON GARLIC POWDER

1 TEASPOON ONION POWDER

2 TABLESPOONS OLIVE OIL

3 LARGE ZUCCHINI (1 POUND)

1 TABLESPOON GHEE

1 SMALL SHALLOT, MINCED (3 TABLESPOONS)

½ CUP CHICKEN STOCK (PAGE 270)

FOR THE SALSA

2 RIPE PEACHES, UNPEELED AND DICED (ABOUT 2 CUPS)

2 TABLESPOONS CHIFFONADED BASIL (SEE PAGE 80)

1 SMALL SHALLOT, MINCED (3 TABLESPOONS)

JUICE OF ½ LIME (2 TABLESPOONS)

1 TEASPOON SALT

1 TEASPOON FRESHLY GROUND BLACK PEPPER

1 TEASPOON GARLIC POWDER

1 TABLESPOON OLIVE OIL

Preheat the oven to 375°F.

In a large bowl, mix together the pork, lamb, 1 tablespoon of the salt, the pepper, garlic powder, onion powder, and olive oil. Form the mixture into 2-ounce balls about 1½ inches in diameter and space evenly on a sheet pan. Roast for 12 to 16 minutes, or until the internal temp reaches 150°F.

While the meatballs roast, make the zucchini noodles: Take a long thin slice off of each zucchini and roll them onto the flat surface you've just made. Cut them lengthwise into slices ⅛-inch thick, then stack the slices and repeat, creating julienned "noodles."

In a large sauté pan, heat the ghee over medium-high heat. After 4 minutes, add the shallot and ½ teaspoon of the salt. Let cook for 3 to 4 minutes, then add the zucchini noodles. Toss in the remaining ½ teaspoon of salt and stir gently. Let sauté for 3 to 4 minutes, then add the stock. Reduce over high heat for about 2 minutes, remove from heat, and set aside.

In a medium bowl, combine all the ingredients for the peach and basil salsa. Refrigerate for at least 2 hours before serving. The salsa will keep for 5 days in the fridge.

To serve, plate the zucchini noodles and top with the meatballs, then ladle on the salsa.

THAI GINGER PORK SAUSAGE

SERVES 4 • COOK TIME 10 MINUTES

INGREDIENTS

1 POUND GROUND PORK

4 TEASPOONS SALT

3 TO 4 THAI BASIL LEAVES, CHIFFONADED (2 TO 3 TABLESPOONS)

1½ TEASPOONS FINELY MINCED GARLIC

1½ TEASPOONS SEEDED, MINCED THAI CHILES (IF YOU DON'T HAVE FRESH YOU CAN USE DRIED)

1 TEASPOON FRESHLY GRATED GINGER

Preheat the oven to 375°F.

Combine all ingredients in a large bowl and mix well. Form the sausage mixture into 2-ounce patties.

Heat a large, thick-bottomed sauté pan or a cast iron pan over medium-high heat. Sear the sausages for 1 minute on each side, for a total of 3 minutes. Place the pan in the oven and cook for 7 minutes.

To chiffonade the basil, stack the leaves on top of the other and roll them up tightly, like a cigar, from top to bottom. Holding the "cigar" from the side and using a very sharp knife, cut the basil crosswise into very thin strips.

PORK PASTOR

SERVES 3 TO 4 • COOK TIME 12 MINUTES, PLUS 8 TO 24 HOURS TO MARINATE

This dish is usually made over an open flame, and the browning of the meat is a key part of the flavor of the dish. A cast iron frying pan will give you the same result on your stovetop, but make sure your pan is dry and very hot. This pork mixture is traditionally served in corn tortillas with a mix of cilantro, onions, and lime. Today we served it in butter lettuce wraps. It's also great on a salad or with cauliflower rice.

In a medium bowl, combine all the ingredients, massaging the seasoning into the pork. Cover and allow to marinate 8 to 24 hours in the refrigerator.

Heat a large, dry cast iron frying pan over medium-high heat. Do not add any oil. Once the pan is hot, add all of the marinated pork mixture. Cook for 10 to 12 minutes, stirring only a couple times. (Minimal stirring will help you develop a nice browning on the meat.)

INGREDIENTS

1¼ POUNDS PORK LOIN, CUT INTO ½-INCH PIECES

1 TEASPOON SALT

1 TEASPOON CHILI POWDER

½ TEASPOON GROUND CUMIN

½ TEASPOON GARLIC POWDER

½ TEASPOON FRESHLY GROUND BLACK PEPPER

1 MEDIUM JALAPEÑO PEPPER (ABOUT 1 OUNCE), SEEDED AND CHOPPED

3½ OUNCES PINEAPPLE, CUT INTO ¼-INCH DICE (1 CUP)

1 TABLESPOON OLIVE OIL

POACHED SEA BASS WITH PAN-SEARED MAITAKE, BOK CHOY, AND DAIKON NOODLES

SERVES 4 · COOK TIME 1 HOUR, PLUS 1 HOUR 20 MINUTES TO MAKE THE POACHING BROTH

INGREDIENTS

FOR THE MAITAKE AND KOMBU POACHING BROTH (YIELD: 2 QUARTS)

3 BUNCHES MAITAKE MUSHROOMS (12 OUNCES), OR OYSTER OR STEMMED SHIITAKE MUSHROOMS

8 CUPS WATER

2 STRIPS DRIED KOMBU SEAWEED

1 CUP BONITO FLAKES

FOR THE DAIKON NOODLES

1 MEDIUM DAIKON RADISH (½ POUND)

½ TABLESPOON PEELED AND GRATED FRESH GINGER

2 TABLESPOONS CHOPPED FRESH CILANTRO

3 TABLESPOONS TOASTED SESAME OIL

ZEST OF 1 LIME

JUICE OF 1 LIME

½ TEASPOON SALT

FOR THE PAN-SEARED MAITAKE MUSH-ROOMS AND BOK CHOY

RESERVED MAITAKE MUSHROOMS FROM BROTH

1 TABLESPOON OLIVE OIL

¼ TEASPOON SALT

7 HEADS BABY BOK CHOY (10 OUNCES TOTAL)

8 CUPS WATER

1 TABLESPOON AVOCADO OIL

1 TABLESPOON GHEE

2 CLOVES GARLIC, THINLY SLICED

¾ CUP MAITAKE AND KOMBU BROTH

This dish is complex, and if you're a beginner, you may find it challenging. You can tackle it for sure, but review the method a few times before starting. If you're short on time, you can make the broth the day before and warm it up over low heat before serving. In fact, the broth can be frozen for up to six months, and it makes a perfect base for any type of Asian soup.

FOR THE SEA BASS

4 CUPS MAITAKE AND KOMBU BROTH

3 TEASPOONS SALT

½ TEASPOON FISH SAUCE, SUCH AS RED BOAT FISH SAUCE

1½ POUNDS SEA BASS OR GROUPER FILLETS, SKIN ON (SEE NOTE)

* Note: When purchasing the sea bass, make sure to buy it with the skin on—it helps the fillets hold together while poaching.

MAKE THE POACHING BROTH

Trim the bottoms off the maitake mushroom clusters. You want to cut right above where you see the individual mushrooms sprouting from the base; this way the mushrooms will naturally separate from each other. Remove the mushroom tops from the base and set them aside in a bowl.

In a large saucepan, place the water, kombu, and maitake bottoms and bring to a bare simmer over medium-low heat. Continue to cook, uncovered, for 1 hour over low heat; do not let it come to a boil. After 1 hour add the bonito flakes and remove from the heat. Allow to sit for 20 minutes and then strain the broth and discard the solids.

MAKE THE DAIKON NOODLES

Peel and discard the outer layer of the daikon radish. Continue to peel with a vegetable peeler to produce thin, flat noodles. Toss the noodles with the ginger, cilantro, sesame oil, lime zest, lime juice, and salt, and allow to marinate in the refrigerator while you complete the rest of your prep.

MAKE THE PAN-SEARED MAITAKE AND BOK CHOY

Preheat the oven to 400°F.

Place the mushroom tops on a sheet pan and lightly toss them in the olive oil and salt. Roast in the oven for 20 to 25 minutes.

It's important to grate ginger against the grain—that is, perpendicular to the length of the root. You will notice a significant increase in aroma when it is grated across the grain. Also, when peeling ginger, use a small spoon to scrape off the skin. Yep, a spoon—just try it.

Oven roasting the mushrooms before finishing them on the stovetop makes them release their water, so you can achieve a deep brown color in the cast iron frying pan.

While the mushrooms are roasting, prep the bok choy: You do not need to wash the bok choy; it will be blanched and placed in an ice bath, so it will be cleaned along the way. To prep the bok choy, slice off the very bottom and quarter it, creating an "X" on the bottom with your knife. Slice upward from the bottom approximately 2 to 3 inches, then gently pull the remaining top portion apart with your hands.

In a medium saucepan over high heat, bring the water to a boil. Prepare a large ice bath and keep it next to the stove. Place the quartered bok choy in the boiling water and blanch for 2 minutes, or until the bok choy is "knife soft." Immediately place it in the ice bath and let it chill for at least 2 minutes. Pull the bok choy from the ice bath, place it on a layer of paper towels, and pat dry.

Heat a large cast iron frying pan over high heat and add the avocado oil. Once the oil is hot, about 2 minutes, add the bok choy quarters. Do not stir—you want to get a nice brown color. Cook for 3 minutes, then add the maitake mushrooms and reduce the heat to medium-high. Add a pinch of salt to the pan and cook for 3 minutes. Add the ghee and garlic, gently stir once, and cook for 3 to 5 minutes. Deglaze the pan with the broth and remove from the heat. Serve hot.

POACH THE SEA BASS

Place enough maitake and kombu broth to cover the fish, about 4 cups, in a large pot. Add the salt and fish sauce and bring to a low simmer—not a boil.

Cut the sea bass into four 6-ounce pieces. Gently place the fish skin side down into the simmering broth. Poach the fish for 3 minutes, covered, and remove from the heat. Allow the fish to cook in the poaching liquid for 3 more minutes—it will continue to cook even though it's off the heat—then remove the skin.

When everything is ready to serve, pull the daikon noodles out of the fridge and place equal portions in four bowls. Place the cooked fish on top of the noodles and top with the pan-seared maitake and bok choy. Finally, ladle broth over the whole dish, filling the bowl.

STUFFED ANAHEIM CHILES

SERVES 2 TO 4 • COOK TIME 40 MINUTES

For this recipe, you can use smaller chiles for appetizers or large bell peppers for an entrée. The filling also makes a great chorizo.

INGREDIENTS

FOR THE FILLING

2 TABLESPOONS OLIVE OIL

½ SMALL YELLOW ONION, DICED (1 CUP)

½ CUP DICED BELL PEPPER, ANY COLOR

1 POUND GROUND PORK

1 TEASPOON FRESHLY GROUND BLACK PEPPER

½ TEASPOON GARLIC POWDER

1 TEASPOON PAPRIKA

1 TEASPOON SMOKED PAPRIKA

1 TEASPOON SALT

6 MEDIUM ANAHEIM OR POBLANO CHILES OR 4 LARGE RED BELL PEPPERS

4 TABLESPOONS SLICED SCALLIONS, FOR GARNISH

Preheat the oven to 325°F.

In a large sauté pan, heat the oil over medium heat. Add the onion and sauté for 4 minutes. Add the diced bell pepper, stir well, and cook for 1 minute. Add the pork, black pepper, garlic powder, paprika, smoked paprika, and salt and stir well. Continue to cook over medium heat for 8 to 10 minutes, or until the pork is cooked through so there is no pink in the meat. Taste and adjust the salt and pepper as needed. You want the mixture to have a kick and a good amount of salt as the seasoning will get diluted while it bakes in the pepper.

Wash the chiles, cut off the tops, and pull out the seeds and any white membranes.

Stuff each Anaheim chile with ¼ cup of the meat mixture, packing it in well. If you're using bell peppers, you should get close to ½ cup of the meat mixture per bell pepper.

Place the stuffed chiles on a sheet pan and oven roast for 25 minutes.

Garnish with sliced scallions before serving.

PULLED CREOLE BRAISED CHICKEN

SERVES 4 • COOK TIME 1 HOUR

INGREDIENTS

1 (4-POUND) CHICKEN, BROKEN DOWN INTO PARTS (SEE PAGE 21), OR 2½ POUNDS BONE-IN, SKIN-ON CHICKEN PIECES

1¼ CUPS CHICKEN STOCK (PAGE 270) OR WATER

½ TEASPOON DRIED THYME

1 TEASPOON DRIED OREGANO

½ TEASPOON ONION POWDER

½ TEASPOON PAPRIKA

¼ TEASPOON CAYENNE PEPPER

½ TEASPOON FRESHLY GROUND BLACK PEPPER

½ TEASPOON FILÉ POWDER

1 TEASPOON SALT

Preheat the oven to 375°F.

Place all the ingredients in an oven-safe 9-by-13-inch pan. Mix everything together well—clean hands are the best tool for this—and cover with a lid or foil. Bake for 1 hour, allow to cool for 10 to 15 minutes, and pull the meat from the bone. This should yield 2½ pounds of pulled chicken.

OKRA BRUNSWICK STEW

SERVES 6 · COOK TIME 55 MINUTES

INGREDIENTS

3 TABLESPOONS OLIVE OIL

1 LARGE YELLOW ONION (14 OUNCES), CUT INTO MEDIUM DICE

SALT, ADDED A PINCH AT A TIME THROUGHOUT THE COOKING PROCESS

1 MEDIUM GREEN BELL PEPPER (9 OUNCES), ROUGHLY CHOPPED

1 MEDIUM RED BELL PEPPER (9 OUNCES), ROUGHLY CHOPPED

½ POUND OKRA, SLICED (2 CUPS)

2 POUNDS TOMATOES, CHOPPED (5 CUPS)

2 CLOVES GARLIC, ROUGHLY CHOPPED

FOR THE CREOLE SPICE

1 TEASPOON PAPRIKA

1 TEASPOON GARLIC POWDER

1 TEASPOON BLACK PEPPER

1 TEASPOON ONION POWDER

1 TEASPOON DRIED OREGANO

4 CUPS CHICKEN STOCK (PAGE 270)

½ TEASPOON FILÉ POWDER

1½ POUNDS PULLED CREOLE BRAISED CHICKEN (PAGE 90)

● ● ●

Heat a thick-bottomed stockpot over medium heat. While cooking this dish, stir every so often as you add the veggies, but don't stir continuously.

Add the oil to the hot pan. Once the oil is hot, add the onion and a pinch of salt and sauté for 3 minutes. Add the peppers and a pinch of salt and sauté for 5 minutes. Add the okra and a pinch of salt and sauté for 7 minutes. Add the tomatoes, garlic, and a pinch of salt and sauté for 10 minutes.

In a small bowl, combine the ingredients for the Creole spice. Add the spice and stock to the pan, stir well, and boil for 30 minutes over medium-high heat. Add the filé powder, stir well, and fold in the pulled chicken. Taste and add additional salt if needed.

In this recipe a pinch of salt is added several times during the cooking process. Here's why: The key to good stews is to have all the flavors come together, and every time you add a tiny bit of salt it denatures the ingredient's cells, which causes the ingredient to release moisture and with it flavor, allowing all the flavors to emerge throughout the cooking process.

SHRIMP WITH GRAPES AND ZUCCHINI NOODLES

SERVES 4 • COOK TIME 10 MINUTES

INGREDIENTS

4 TABLESPOONS GHEE OR BACON FAT, DIVIDED

½ CUP PLUS 2 TABLESPOONS MINCED SHALLOTS, DIVIDED

2 CUPS GRAPES, HALVED AND SEEDED

3 CUPS GRAPE TOMATOES, HALVED

4 CUPS ZUCCHINI NOODLES (2 POUNDS ZUCCHINI TOTAL)

1 TABLESPOON FRESH MARJORAM LEAVES, PLUS ADDITIONAL FOR GARNISH

¾ CUP SHRIMP STOCK (PAGE 272), DIVIDED

1 TEASPOON FRESHLY GROUND BLACK PEPPER

1½ POUNDS JUMBO (U15) SHRIMP, PEELED AND DEVEINED (RESERVE THE SHELLS FOR STOCK)

½ TEASPOON SALT

Shrimp with the shell on are typically fresher—it's not a guarantee, but it's a good sign, and you get the shells, which make great stock (see page 272 for a recipe). Having to peel the shrimp means a little more work, but there's a reward.

All shrimp are rated according to size. The ratings vary by region, but in general, if a number is given, it indicates how many shrimp are in a pound—so the bigger the number, the smaller the shrimp. If "U" appears in the rating, as in "U15," it stands for "under"; in that case, there are fewer than fifteen shrimp in a pound, so each shrimp is at least 1 ounce. One and a half pounds of jumbo (U15) shrimp will, on average, feed four people five shrimp each, with a few left over.

SIZE	NUMBER OF SHRIMP PER POUND
Colossal	Fewer than 10
Jumbo	11–15
Extra large	16–20
Large	21–30
Medium	31–35
Small	36–45
Miniature	100

To make the zucchini noodles, you can use a julienne blade on a mandoline or a spiralizer, but I like to cut them by hand. It's a great way to practice your knife skills, but it does takes much longer than using the tools.

Heat 2 tablespoons of the ghee in a large sauté pan over medium-high heat. Once the ghee is hot, add ½ cup of the shallots, the grapes, tomatoes, zucchini noodles, and marjoram. Let it cook for 1 minute, then add ¼ cup of the stock, turn the heat to high, and cook for 3 minutes. You don't want the vegetables to develop much color. After 3 minutes, the liquid should have reduced a lot but won't be completely gone. Add the black pepper, remove the mixture from the pan, and set aside.

Wipe the pan with a paper towel and put it back over high heat. Dust the shrimp with the salt. Melt the remaining 2 tablespoons of ghee in the pan and add the remaining 2 tablespoons of shallots and the shrimp. As soon as the shallots start to brown (this will happen quickly), add ¼ cup of the stock, which will also release the shrimp. Cook for 1 minute and add the remaining ¼ cup of stock. Play it by ear; if the shrimp needs to cook a bit more, add a little more stock. Be careful not to overcook it, though—overcooked shrimp is close to unchewable.

Remove from heat, divide the vegetable mixture into bowls, and top with the shrimp and the desired amount of stock. Garnish with fresh marjoram.

BEER BUTT CHICKEN

SERVES 8 · COOK TIME 45 MINUTES

INGREDIENTS

FOR THE DRY RUB

3 TABLESPOONS KOSHER SALT

2 TABLESPOONS FRESHLY GROUND BLACK PEPPER

2 TABLESPOONS GARLIC POWDER

1 TABLESPOON CHILI POWDER

1 TABLESPOON ONION POWDER

2 (12-OUNCE) CANS HARD CIDER

2 (3-POUND) CHICKENS

Combine all dry rub ingredients in a bowl and mix well.

Place 2 cups of wood chips (I prefer hickory or pecan; never use a soft wood like pine) in a 6-by-6-inch or 7-by-7-inch aluminum pan. Soak with one-third (about 4 ounces) of the cider from both cans. Let sit for 1 hour, then drain.

While the wood chips are soaking, massage the chickens with the dry rub. There's no need to be perfect here, but the more evenly the rub is applied, the more perfectly seasoned the skin that you'll be fighting over.

Arrange the charcoal on one side of the grill and light it. Once it is almost ready, place the wood chips in the foil pan directly over the charcoal. Place one can of hard cider up each chicken's back end and set each chicken in an empty foil pan. Place the birds on the other side of the grill from the wood chips and charcoal. Cover the grill and let it do its thing for 35 to 40 minutes.

Use a pair of tongs to grab the can and another pair to grab the bird, and pull the bird off the can. Be careful, as there will be steam coming from the cans. Put the birds on a cutting board and let rest for 20 minutes. Carve or pull off the meat, and save the bones for stock.

This recipe can also be cooked in the oven, sans smoking. Put the chicken, standing up, in a roasting pan on the bottom rack of the oven and cook at 375°F for 45 to 50 minutes.

BRAISED PORK AND BARBECUE SAUCE

SERVES 12 · COOK TIME 3½ HOURS

INGREDIENTS

FOR THE BRAISED PORK

8 POUNDS PORK BUTT, CUT INTO LARGE, ½- TO 1-POUND CHUNKS

1 (12-OUNCE) CAN HARD APPLE CIDER

6 CUPS DILUTED CHICKEN STOCK (3 CUPS WATER, 3 CUPS STOCK) (PAGE 270)

6 OUNCES TOMATO PASTE

3 TABLESPOONS MAPLE SYRUP

3 TABLESPOONS STONE-GROUND MUSTARD

3 TABLESPOONS APPLE CIDER VINEGAR

1½ TABLESPOONS SALT

1 TEASPOON FRESHLY GROUND BLACK PEPPER

FOR THE BARBECUE SAUCE

1¼ TO 1½ CUPS APPLE CIDER

12 OUNCES TOMATO PASTE

1 LARGE SHALLOT, MINCED

¾ CUP APPLE CIDER VINEGAR

½ CUP MAPLE SYRUP

4 TABLESPOONS STONE-GROUND MUSTARD

2 TEASPOONS SALT

1 TEASPOON FRESHLY GROUND BLACK PEPPER

1 TEASPOON GARLIC POWDER

½ TEASPOON PAPRIKA

¼ TEASPOON GROUND CUMIN

This recipe feeds a lot of people, making it perfect for a weekend barbecue—or you could just make it for yourself and have leftovers in your fridge for the week. The barbecue sauce is a South Carolina–style, red mustard–based sauce.

Preheat the oven to 325°F.

Combine all the braised pork ingredients in a large braising pan. Mix well, making sure the tomato paste is mixed in. Cover and braise in the oven for 3 hours.

While the pork braises, make the barbecue sauce: Place the apple cider in a medium saucepan over medium heat and reduce by half. Add the remaining ingredients and simmer for 15 to 20 minutes.

Transfer the mixture to a blender (preferably high-speed) and blend to a silky smooth texture.

Remove the pork from the oven and allow to cool for 30 minutes. Remove the fat from the top and pull off the meat.

Toss the pulled meat in the barbecue sauce and serve with Collard Greens (page 102) and Chive Mashed Potatoes (page 170).

GARLICKY BURGERS OVER SWEET POTATO HASH

SERVES 4 · COOK TIME 20 MINUTES

INGREDIENTS

FOR THE HASH

2 TABLESPOONS COCONUT OIL OR AVOCADO OIL

1 YELLOW ONION, SLICED

1 RED BELL PEPPER, SLICED

2 LARGE SWEET POTATOES, PEELED AND CUT INTO ½-INCH DICE

SALT AND PEPPER

1½ POUNDS GROUND BEEF, BISON, OR ELK

3 CLOVES GARLIC, SMASHED AND MINCED

½ TABLESPOON SALT

½ TABLESPOON FRESHLY GROUND BLACK PEPPER

1 TABLESPOON AVOCADO OIL, COCONUT OIL, OR OLIVE OIL

SPICY ASIAN SLAW (PAGE 225), TO SERVE

1 LARGE AVOCADO, SLICED, TO SERVE

If you plan to grill the burgers, preheat the grill.

To make the hash: Heat the oil in a large cast iron pan over medium heat. Add the onion and bell pepper and sauté till soft, about 6 minutes. Add the sweet potatoes and brown until cooked through, about 10 to 12 minutes. Salt and pepper to taste. Once the potatoes are cooked, you can keep them warm over low heat until you are ready to serve.

While the hash cooks, in a large bowl combine the ground meat, garlic, salt, black pepper, and avocado oil. Mix well and form a small test patty.

Grill the test patty or cook it in a cast iron pan for 4 minutes per side (for medium-rare burgers). Taste and adjust the seasoning if necessary, then form the remaining meat mixture into four equal-size patties and cook or grill.

Plate the sweet potato hash and top with a burger, Spicy Asian Slaw (page 225), and the avocado slices. If you're really hungry, add a fried egg on there, too!

COLLARD GREENS

SERVES 8 • COOK TIME 1 TO 3 HOURS

INGREDIENTS

6 OUNCES SUGAR-FREE CURED (NOT BRINED) BACON, DICED

1 MEDIUM YELLOW ONION, JULIENNED

4 BUNCHES COLLARDS, STEMMED AND CUT INTO 1-INCH STRIPS

2 TABLESPOONS APPLE CIDER VINEGAR

Place the bacon in a large, cold saucepot and heat over medium-high heat. Cook until the bacon is crispy (keep all the rendered bacon fat in the pan). Add the onion and cook for 3 minutes. Add the collards and vinegar, reduce the heat to low, cover, and simmer for 1 to 3 hours. Stir every 30 minutes or so. The longer you cook collards, the better they get.

ARTICHOKE, OLIVE, AND TOMATO DIP

SERVES 20 AS A DIP OR 6 AS A SIDE

This dish is great on its own as a side, but it's also perfect for topping a salad. You can also use it as a dip with crudités, and it's amazing with pastured pork rinds.

INGREDIENTS

1 (14-OUNCE) CAN ARTICHOKE HEARTS

1 (14-OUNCE) CAN WHOLE SAN MARZANO TOMATOES OR 1 POUND FRESH SAN MARZANOS

⅓ CUP PITTED KALAMATA OLIVES

2 TABLESPOONS FRESH PARSLEY

1 TO 2 CLOVES GARLIC

SALT, IF NEEDED

In a food processor or by hand, roughly chop the artichoke hearts and tomatoes, discarding any extra liquid. If you use a food processor, process the artichoke hearts and tomatoes separately. Roughly chop the Kalamata olives by hand, then roughly chop the parsley and garlic.

Mix all the ingredients in a bowl, stirring well. Allow to marinate for a couple hours before serving. Taste and add salt if needed. Every brand of canned vegetables has a different amount of added salt, so you may or may not need to add more.

EGGPLANT DIP

SERVES 12 • COOK TIME 40 MINUTES

INGREDIENTS

4 TO 6 TABLESPOONS OLIVE OIL, DIVIDED

1 SMALL YELLOW ONION, ROUGHLY CHOPPED

½ TEASPOON SALT, DIVIDED, PLUS MORE TO TASTE

1 VERY LARGE OR 2 MEDIUM ITALIAN EGGPLANTS
(ABOUT 1 POUND), CUT INTO 1-INCH CUBES

½ TEASPOON GARAM MASALA

FRESHLY GROUND BLACK PEPPER

¼ CUP ROUGHLY CHOPPED FRESH PARSLEY OR CHIVES

In a large sauté pan, heat 2 tablespoons of the olive oil over medium-high heat. Add the onion and ¼ teaspoon of the salt and cook until caramelized, 8 to 10 minutes. Add the eggplant and the remaining ¼ teaspoon of the salt and cook until the eggplant is golden-brown and soft in the center, 30 minutes or so.

Transfer the eggplant mixture to a food processor and lightly process, adding the garam masala and the remaining 2 to 4 tablespoons of the olive oil (2 tablespoons yields a thicker mixture while 4 makes it creamier). Do not overdo it in the food processor; you want to keep the eggplant a little chunky. Chill in the refrigerator, add salt and pepper to taste, and fold in the fresh parsley or chives before serving.

BURST TOMATO SAUCE

YIELD 4 CUPS · COOK TIME 15 MINUTES

This sauce is amazing on spaghetti squash, as well as with roasted okra and mushrooms. It freezes very well, so it's perfect for making large batches during the summer to enjoy during the colder months.

INGREDIENTS

½ CUP OLIVE OIL

1 MEDIUM YELLOW ONION (8 OUNCES), ROUGHLY CHOPPED INTO 1-INCH PIECES

3 MEDIUM TOMATOES (1½ POUNDS), ROUGHLY CHOPPED INTO 2-INCH PIECES

¾ TEASPOON SALT

2 SMALL CLOVES GARLIC, ROUGHLY CHOPPED

¼ CUP FRESH BASIL LEAVES, TORN

Add the oil to a stockpot and heat over medium-high heat. Add the onion and sauté until soft, about 8 to 10 minutes. Increase the heat to high and wait 1 minute. Once you start to see the onions brown on the side of the pot and the pot is super hot, add the tomatoes and salt, carefully stir, and step back—the tomatoes will burst and magically melt to a delicate consistency in about 1 minute. (If your pot isn't hot enough, the tomatoes may not burst and dissolve as quickly. In that case, continue cooking up to 5 minutes more, and eventually they will dissolve.) Add the garlic, sauté for 2 minutes, and remove from heat. Fold in the basil and season to taste.

A little note on fresh garlic: You always want to add it at the end because it has no water and therefore burns very quickly.

SMASHED PLANTAINS

SERVES 4 • COOK TIME 15 MINUTES

Smashed plantains are great on their own, but they're also an ideal vessel for dips and spreads. We like to dip them in Chimichurri Sauce (page 252).

You're going to need some extra equipment for this recipe: a large cast iron pan or large, thick-bottomed saucepan for frying, a small sauté pan to smash the plantains, and a sheet pan lined with paper towels.

INGREDIENTS

1 CUP AVOCADO OIL

3 PLANTAINS, PEELED AND CUT INTO 1½-INCH-THICK SLICES

SALT

Warm the avocado oil in a cast iron pan for 6 minutes on medium heat. Using a pair of tongs, place all the plantain slices in the pan starting at the 12 o'clock position and working clockwise so you can keep track of which ones went in first. When they begin to turn golden-brown, after about 2 minutes, start again at the 12 o'clock position and flip them over and cook for another 2 minutes. Remove from the pan and set on a sheet pan lined with paper towels. Leave the cast iron pan with the oil on the stovetop and turn the heat down to low.

After the plantains have cooled, about 4 minutes, gently smash them with a small sauté pan to about ¼ inch thick, pushing straight down. Don't push too hard or they will separate.

Turn the heat under the oil back up to medium and fry the smashed plantains for 2 to 3 minutes per side. Transfer back to the paper towels and sprinkle liberally with salt. Cool before serving.

EGG AND FRUIT HASH

SERVES 4 · COOK TIME 5 MINUTES

You can make this with any vegetables, and it's a great way to use leftovers. We used leftover beets, avocados, and Brussels sprouts from dinner the night before.

INGREDIENTS

1 TABLESPOON GHEE, DIVIDED

2 CUPS COOKED VEGETABLES

2 PINCHES OF SALT, DIVIDED, PLUS MORE TO TASTE

8 EGGS

2 CUPS FRESH FRUIT (I LIKE STRAWBERRIES AND PEACHES WITH SOME PINEAPPLE)

In a sauté pan, heat ½ tablespoon of the ghee over medium-high heat for 3 minutes. Add the vegetables and a pinch of salt and stir.

In a separate sauté pan, heat the remaining ½ tablespoon of ghee over high heat. Cook the eggs over easy or scrambled, two at a time, with a pinch of salt. We prefer over easy; it's nice to plate them on top of the veggies so you can break the yolk on them.

Plate the eggs with equal portions of the fruit and veggies and serve.

GRILLED AVOCADO, PORTOBELLO, AND RED ONION SALAD

SERVES 4 · COOK TIME 10 MINUTES

INGREDIENTS

3 MEDIUM AVOCADOS (6 TO 7 OUNCES EACH), PITTED AND HALVED, PEEL ON

5 SMALL OR 2 LARGE PORTOBELLO MUSHROOMS, STEMMED (8 OUNCES TOTAL)

2 TABLESPOONS OLIVE OIL

2 TEASPOONS SALT

1 TEASPOON FRESHLY GROUND BLACK PEPPER

½ RED ONION OR 1 TO 2 SHALLOTS (4 TO 5 OUNCES TOTAL), SHAVED

2 TABLESPOONS CHOPPED FRESH PARSLEY

2 TEASPOONS BALSAMIC VINEGAR

Give the grill a quick coat of oil and heat until it's very hot. Sear the avocados face down for 1 minute, rotate 90 degrees, and sear for 1 minute more, creating hash marks. Remove from heat.

Grill the portobellos for 2 minutes, rotate 90 degrees, and sear for 1 to 2 minutes more. Flip the mushrooms and repeat, for a total cooking time of 6 to 8 minutes. You may need to add or subtract a couple minutes depending on the size of the mushrooms and how hot your grill gets. Be careful not to overcook the mushrooms; they should be just tender and charred, but if you overcook them, they will get slimy.

Carefully slice the avocados and mushrooms to be close to equal in size, roughly 1 inch square, and scoop out the avocado pieces from the peel. Add the mushrooms to a bowl and coat with the olive oil, salt, pepper, shaved onion, and parsley. Carefully fold in the avocados and drizzle with the balsamic vinegar.

GRILLED CANTALOUPE AND EGGPLANT SALAD

SERVES 4 · COOK TIME 35 MINUTES

INGREDIENTS

1 SMALL TO MEDIUM CANTALOUPE (2 POUNDS; SEE NOTE)

1 LARGE ITALIAN EGGPLANT (1¼ POUNDS)

¼ CUP OLIVE OIL

¾ TEASPOON SALT, DIVIDED

⅛ TEASPOON FRESHLY GROUND BLACK PEPPER

½ YELLOW ONION

¼ CUP FRESH MINT LEAVES

1 TEASPOON ORANGE ZEST

Note: When picking a cantaloupe, choose one that's firm to the touch, feels heavy for its size, and has a noticeable fruit aroma.

Preheat the oven to 400°F and preheat an outdoor grill or cast iron stovetop grill to high heat.

Cut off the outer rind of the cantaloupe, slice in half, and remove the seeds, then cut into 2-inch-thick slices. Wipe down the grill with an old but clean kitchen towel that has been dabbed in olive oil and place the melon slices on the hot grill. Cook for about 2 minutes on each side—just long enough to develop defined and dark char marks without overcooking the melon. Do not move the cantaloupe while grilling; only touch it to flip. If you see the cantaloupe falling apart on the grill, you've cooked it too long.

Cut the eggplant into 1-by 3-inch sticks and place on a sheet pan. Lightly coat with the oil, ½ teaspoon of the salt, and the black pepper and roast in the oven for 30 minutes, or until the eggplant is golden and very tender. Allow the eggplant to cool to room temperature.

Shave the onion on a mandoline or slice very thinly by hand. If the mint leaves are large, gently cut them in half. Stack the leaves on top of each other and, using a sharp knife, gently cut down the middle, or chiffonade into thin strips.

In a bowl, gently mix together the grilled cantaloupe, eggplant, raw onion, mint, orange zest, and the remaining ¼ teaspoon of salt and serve. This salad is great the next day as the flavors marinate together beautifully.

FENNEL AND TOMATO SALAD

SERVES 4 TO 6

INGREDIENTS

1 POUND HEIRLOOM TOMATOES

2 TO 3 SMALL SHALLOTS (4 OUNCES TOTAL)

1 TEASPOON LEMON ZEST

1 TABLESPOON LEMON JUICE OR APPLE CIDER VINEGAR

1 TABLESPOON OLIVE OIL

½ TEASPOON SALT, PLUS MORE TO TASTE

⅛ TEASPOON FRESHLY GROUND BLACK PEPPER

1 POUND FENNEL BULBS WITH FRONDS

Cut the tomatoes into wedges and then cut the wedges into thirds, so that you have triangular bite-sized pieces.

Thinly shave the shallots on a mandoline or slice very finely by hand. Combine the tomatoes, shallots, lemon zest, lemon juice, olive oil, salt, and pepper in a large bowl.

Remove the fronds from the fennel bulbs and roughly chop enough of the fronds to yield 1 cup. Add the chopped fronds to the bowl.

Thinly shave the fennel bulbs on a mandoline or slice thinly with a knife. Immediately add to the bowl and gently mix, making sure the fennel is coated well— the lemon juice in the dressing will protect it from oxidizing and turning brown. Let sit for 20 minutes and then taste; add more salt if needed.

If you want to step this salad up a notch, add smoked trout roe at the very end. It adds texture, temperature, and saltiness. The little cold eggs burst in your mouth with fresh saltiness that cuts through the salad. *Whoa.*

COFFEE ICE CREAM

SERVES 5 • COOK TIME 25 MINUTES, PLUS OVERNIGHT TO COOL

INGREDIENTS

2 (13.5-OUNCE) CANS UNSWEETENED, WHOLE-FAT COCONUT MILK OR COCONUT CREAM

½ CUP HONEY

1 TABLESPOON FLAVORLESS GRASS-FED GELATIN (SEE NOTE)

1 CUP DARK ROAST COFFEE GRINDS

* Note: I like to use Great Lakes Unflavored Beef Gelatin (the one with the orange label).

In a medium saucepot over medium-low heat, warm the coconut milk very slowly so it doesn't separate. Once it gets warm, about 5 minutes, add the honey while whisking.

Continue to heat until the coconut mixture is just below a simmer (180°F), about 10 minutes total. Add the gelatin and whisk until it's fully dissolved.

Once the mixture is at a good simmer (180°F to 195°F), pour it into a French press with the coffee grinds. Give it a good stir and allow to steep for 8 minutes. Strain it through a sieve held over a bowl.

Allow to cool in the fridge overnight. The next day, if the mixture has solidified, allow it to sit at room temperature for 30 minutes.

Pour into an ice cream maker and run for 25 minutes. Eat it right away if you like soft-serve or freeze it overnight for firm, scoopable ice cream. If you do freeze it, let it sit out for 5 to 10 minutes before serving for the perfect texture.

MANGO ICE CREAM

SERVES 5 · COOK TIME 15 MINUTES, PLUS 3 HOURS TO OVERNIGHT TO COOL

INGREDIENTS

2 (13.5-OUNCE) CANS UNSWEETENED, WHOLE-FAT COCONUT MILK OR COCONUT CREAM

½ CUP COCONUT SUGAR CRYSTALS OR HONEY

1 TABLESPOON FLAVORLESS GRASS-FED GELATIN (SEE NOTE)

⅛ CUP COLD WATER

1 RIPE MANGO, DICED

In a medium saucepot over medium-low heat, warm the coconut milk very slowly so it doesn't separate. Once it gets warm, about 5 minutes, add the sugar or honey while whisking.

Bloom the gelatin for 5 minutes in the cold water. Once the coconut mixture is just below a simmer (180°F), about 10 minutes, add the gelatin and whisk until it's fully dissolved.

Place the diced mango in a blender, add the hot coconut mixture, and blend for 20 to 30 seconds. Pour the mixture into a bowl and allow it to cool in the fridge; overnight is best, but at least 3 hours are needed. If the mixture has solidified when you take it out, allow it to sit at room temperature for 30 minutes.

Pour into an ice cream maker and run for 25 minutes. Eat it right away if you like soft-serve or freeze it overnight for firm, scoopable ice cream. If you do freeze it, let it sit out for 5 to 10 minutes before serving for the perfect texture.

* Note: I like to use Great Lakes Unflavored Beef Gelatin.

COOKING THROUGH A CSA BOX

Community Supported Agriculture, or CSA, is a great way to get a variety of fresh, in-season produce directly from farmers. When you purchase a CSA subscription from a local farmer, you receive a box of seasonal produce every week. You're also guaranteeing business for the farmer for the season, which lets them hire more people and plant more crops. Using ingredients from my CSA box, I might whip up a salad of grilled peppers and broccolini tossed with some thinly sliced breakfast radish, shallots, grilled chicken, and crisp radicchio. Dressed with some olive oil and fresh lime juice, it spells local, simple, and delicious. Receiving a weekly box of fresh veggies can quickly become overwhelming, though, if you don't get a handle on the harvest. All you need is some strategy.

The easiest way to show you what to do with a CSA box is to have you look over my shoulder as I assess what's in a box, decide how to store it and what to use first, and turn it into a week's worth of meals.

SORTING AND STORING YOUR VEGGIES

Today we picked up our CSA box from Suzie's Farm at the Ocean Beach farmers market near our house. It's fall here in San Diego, which means semi-chilly nights in the 40s and pleasant days in the 60s to 70s with a decent amount of sun. Today in the basket we have:

- Acorn squash
- Red beets
- Red butter lettuce
- Red Bibb lettuce
- Romaine
- Breakfast or D'Avignon radish
- Cilantro
- Broccolini
- Various chile peppers
- Bean sprouts and lentils
- Kale
- Rainbow chard

What a haul! There are lots of really great things to work with here. First things first: we need to properly store all of these veggies. The acorn squash and beets don't need to be refrigerated, but the beets did come whole with the greens, so those are snipped off and stored in the fridge along with the chard.

All of your salad greens should be kept in a separate drawer somewhere in the middle of the fridge. (Never put salad greens in a bottom drawer that touches the refrigerator wall; the direct contact with something so cold will burn the leaves and ruin them. If you don't have a drawer in the middle of your fridge, just don't use a drawer.) First, cut the greens off at the root and wash and dry them. Then, lightly wrap each type of lettuce in a paper towel and place it in a plastic bag. Store it with the bag open—this helps keep the moisture content perfect, so your lettuce will last as long as possible.

The radish, broccolini, peppers, kale, and chard can all be kept in the crisper drawer in your fridge without any special care. The lentils and bean sprouts are obviously not Paleo, so you can give them to your neighbor. (Or just eat them. I won't tell the Paleo police if you won't.)

RED BEETS

RADISHES

CILANTRO

ROMAINE

CHILE PEPPERS

BEAN SPROUTS AND LENTILS

RAINBOW CHARD

ACORN SQUASH

KALE

RED BUTTER LETTUCE

BROCCOLINI

RED BIBB LETTUCE

DECIDING WHAT TO USE AND HOW

Use the salad greens first because, despite your best efforts, they will only last about four to six days at most. The chard and kale may start to droop a bit but will still cook up great five to six days out. The squash is good for a long, long time; the peppers, for a week or two. I like to try and find uses for the chiles in my weekly prep, but they are one of those items that can certainly add up quick after a couple weeks of CSA deliveries. Try pickling or canning them, or make your own hot sauce.

Throughout the week, make an effort to use some of the vegetables in every meal. If you don't, your CSA box will start to feel like a weight around your neck. Even though the squash will keep, I suggest you tackle it within a couple days; otherwise, it's easy to develop an aversion to it. There are recipes for acorn squash on pages 136 and 140.

But really, all you need to do is this: cut off the top and bottom, slice it in half, scoop out the seeds—acorn squash skin can be eaten, so there's no need to peel it—cut it into ½-inch cubes, toss it in olive oil, sprinkle on some pinches of salt and pepper, and roast at 350°F for about 40 minutes. Toss half the squash in fresh sage and serve it as a side at dinner; toss the other half in an egg scramble a day or two later for breakfast.

Thinly slice the chard and sauté it in oil, add in some sliced radish, peppers, and some of the salad greens, top with leftover meat from the night before, and there's lunch.

Don't be intimidated, and have fun with it. If you screw something up, there will more than likely be more of that same vegetable coming in the next week's box, giving you the chance to get it right—or even better—next time.

How awesome is that? In three months of cooking, you can work your way through almost two dozen different vegetables! And you'll have tasted them at their peak of freshness, just days, not weeks, after they were picked.

Each week there is a new challenge, and it's easy to let it get away from you. You have to set aside some prep time, two if not three times a week, to clean, sort, and prep the veggies so they get used before they go bad. Don't be that person who signs up for a CSA and lets half of it go bad every week. Make a plan with your spouse or roommate to split the work. If you live alone, consider getting a half share or finding a friend to split it with.

If you find you are crunched for prep time or space, you may also be able to get a box every other week rather than weekly. Either way, check out the farms in your area and their CSAs and get started. (A list of CSAs around the country is provided on page 284.)

MAKING THE MOST OF A CSA BOX

Here is a sample of some of the fall harvest vegetables from Suzie's Farm in San Diego:

- Arugula
- Beets
- Cabbage
- Carrots
- Fennel
- Kale
- Lettuce
- Radishes
- Salad greens
- Spinach
- Spring onions
- Swiss chard
- Pumpkins
- Winter squash
- Broccoli
- Peas
- Cauliflower
- Tomatillos
- Shell beans

CAST IRON CHARRED BROCCOLINI

SERVES 4 • COOK TIME 10 MINUTES

INGREDIENTS

2 TABLESPOONS BACON FAT

1 BUNCH BROCCOLINI (APPROXIMATELY 1 POUND),
BOTTOM INCH TRIMMED

¼ TEASPOON PLUS A PINCH OF SALT

1 TABLESPOON CHOPPED GARLIC

½ CUP CHICKEN STOCK (PAGE 270)

4 POACHED EGGS (PAGE 132), TO SERVE (OPTIONAL)

Heat a large cast iron frying pan over high heat; when the pan is very hot—just short of smoking—add the bacon fat. Add the broccolini and ¼ teaspoon of the salt and cook for 2 to 3 minutes without stirring or moving. Turn the broccolini over and cook for 2 to 3 minutes more.

Add the garlic and a pinch of salt and give it another stir. As soon as you see the garlic start to turn brown, after less than a minute, add the chicken stock. Stir a bit. Let the stock reduce and the broccolini cook through for about 3 to 4 minutes. Don't cook the liquid all the way down; you want some of it to remain as a sauce.

Plate the broccolini and finish it with the sauce from the pan. It can be served as-is or topped with a poached egg for a meal.

POACHED EGGS

COOK TIME 2½ TO 3 MINUTES

INGREDIENTS

6 CUPS WATER

2 TABLESPOONS WHITE VINEGAR

EGGS

In a medium saucepan, combine the water and vinegar and bring to just short of a simmer. When you see bubbles just starting to come up from the bottom of the pan, reduce the heat to medium-low. Keep just under or at a bare simmer. The water temperature will be 180°F to 185°F.

Crack each egg into a small ramekin—if you're making multiple eggs, crack each egg individually and poach them one at a time. You will eventually get a feel for this technique and be able to make two or three eggs at a time, but don't jump into that right away. It will turn into a mess and you'll get discouraged, and nobody wants that to happen.

Take a slotted spoon and stir the water 5 to 6 times to get the water moving in a circular motion, like a cyclone. Once the water is spinning, pull the spoon out and count to ten to allow the water to slow to a gentle spin.

With the ramekin just above the water, gently pour the egg into the center of the cyclone. You'll see the egg white start to swirl up and around itself. This is exactly what you are looking for.

You may freak out at first, thinking the egg will stick to the bottom, but leave it alone. In about 2 minutes it will float to the top. Once it has floated to the top, wait 30 to 45 seconds and then pull it out with a slotted spoon. Perfect.

When you're ready to try more than one egg at a time, here are a few tips: It's all about getting your first egg good and set, and then as it forms up you can move it off to the side and very, very, very gently give the water a small stir and add the next egg. You should be taking the first egg out a minute after dropping the third egg in. This is a good method for getting a lot done in a short amount of time.

ROMAINE, RADISH, AND ROASTED BEET SALAD

SERVES 4 • COOK TIME 90 MINUTES TO ROAST THE BEETS

Because the beets have to be roasted ahead of time, this is not a salad that can be whipped together on short notice—although I think that it makes a good argument for keeping big batches of roasted beets on hand. They're great additions to lots of dishes.

INGREDIENTS

1 LARGE HEAD ROMAINE LETTUCE

3 MEDIUM BREAKFAST RADISHES

3 ANAHEIM OR POBLANO CHILES

1 EATING CITRUS OF YOUR CHOICE (GRAPEFRUIT OR BLOOD ORANGE ARE IDEAL)

3 HERB-ROASTED BEETS (PAGE 234)

PINCH OF SALT

PINCH OF FRESHLY GROUND BLACK PEPPER

2 TABLESPOONS OLIVE OIL

4 POACHED EGGS (PAGE 132), TO SERVE

Slice the romaine into 1-inch-wide strips. Wash thoroughly, rinse well, drain, and dry thoroughly. Thinly slice the radishes on a mandoline or by hand.

Slice the Anaheim chiles crosswise into strips and remove the seeds. If you prefer more spice, you can leave the seeds in.

Supreme the citrus: Slice off the very top and the bottom of the fruit and then carefully slice off the peel, following the curve of the fruit, all the way through the pith. This will give you a gem of just the insides. Note the white membranes that separate the citrus into individual segments. Our goal is to get those perfect little wedges of citrus in-between the membranes. With a sharp paring knife and a sure hand, slice parallel to one of the membranes, getting as close to it as you can, clear through to the center of the fruit. Make another slice alongside the membrane on the other side of the fruit segment and remove the segment. Continue working your way around the fruit until all of the segments are removed.

Cut the beets into wedges and then cut the wedges in half, so you have bite-sized pieces.

Plate individually by making a base of romaine and topping it with the beets, radishes, and chiles. Sprinkle with the salt and pepper and drizzle the oil over it. Serve with the citrus wedges and top with a poached egg.

Did you know only mammals taste the heat in chiles? True story. The majority of the heat, which comes from capsaicin, is in the seeds. Anaheims are fairly mild. Poblanos will also work for this recipe, just nothing too hot.

BISON ROULADE WITH PAN-WILTED CHARD

SERVES 2 AS AN ENTRÉE OR 4 AS AN APPETIZER
COOK TIME 15 MINUTES, PLUS 1½ HOURS TO MAKE THE FILLING

INGREDIENTS

FOR THE FILLING

½ SMALL ACORN SQUASH (ABOUT ½ POUND; SEE NOTE)

1 TEASPOON PLUS A PINCH OF SALT, DIVIDED

½ TABLESPOON GHEE

1 SMALL LEEK, FINELY CHOPPED (⅔ CUP)

1 TABLESPOON CHOPPED FRESH PARSLEY

2 (6-OUNCE) BISON SIRLOIN STEAKS

2 PINCHES OF SALT, DIVIDED

½ BUNCH RAINBOW CHARD

2 TABLESPOONS BACON FAT

2 TABLESPOONS THINLY SLICED GREEN ONIONS OR FRESH HERB OF YOUR CHOICE, FOR GARNISH

To blow people away at a dinner party, serve a few slices of roulade as an appetizer before an elegant multicourse meal. This isn't the easiest dish to pull off—I made quite a few bad roulades before I had it down—but man, is it delicious, gorgeous, and sure to impress. To make this feat a bit easier, the puree in this recipe can be done a day in advance.

Butterflying the steaks helps you get them as thin as possible with minimal pounding. My advice is to take your time, have a steady hand, and adopt a "measure twice, cut once" attitude.

The acorn squash and leek puree was developed as the filling for this dish, but it also works well as a side; just double the amounts to serve four. If you're in a hurry, you could serve it with bison burgers to have all the same flavors and nutrition as the roulade without all the work.

The best part of this recipe is the smell of the leeks sautéing in ghee. Few things make me more sure of my career choice in life than the smell of leeks in ghee or butter.

* Note: Because this squash came from a CSA box—instead of traveling across the country and sitting in storage before arriving at a supermarket and then making its way into your kitchen—it has a distinct flavor that's a bit richer and slightly nuttier, and it's filled with more vitamins and minerals, the things that sustain you.

Peeling acorn squash may be one of the more thankless tasks in a kitchen. It has a thick skin and can be tough to work with. I recommend using Swiss-made vegetable peelers—they are a thousand times better than other vegetable peelers. Kuhn is my favorite brand, and they cost just $4.

MAKE THE FILLING

Peel and seed the acorn squash and cut it into 1-inch pieces. Remember to create a flat surface for cutting (see more on that on page 128).

Put the squash in a small saucepan and add just enough water to cover it. Add 1 teaspoon of the salt and bring to a boil over medium-high heat, then cover and continue to boil for 25 minutes. The squash will become tender and most of the water will evaporate. Strain over a bowl to remove any remaining water and reserve the water in case it's needed for pureeing. Puree with an immersion blender, adding a little of the reserved cooking water if needed.

Heat a sauté pan over medium heat. Add the ghee and, once it's melted, add the leek and the remaining pinch of salt. This is more of a sweat than a sauté. Sweat for 3 to 4 minutes, stirring often, just until the leeks are softened through but not browned. Remove from the heat.

In a bowl, combine the pureed squash with the leek and chopped parsley. Place in the fridge to chill for 1 hour, which will make it easier to fill and wrap the roulade. (If serving as a side dish, serve warm.)

To sweat something is to cook it in fat, like a sauté, using a sauté pan, but at a slightly lower temperature than a sauté. This brings flavors together a little more slowly and doesn't cook the ingredients down so much, leaving their textures more intact and, in the case of vegetables, keeping them less sweet.

MAKE THE ROULADE AND PREP THE CHARD

Preheat the oven to 375°F.

To butterfly the steaks, start on one side and slowly slice horizontally through the middle of each one, gently pulling the top part open as you cut to keep the cut even and in the middle of the steak. Stop before you get all the way through.

Lay out a piece of plastic wrap on a large flat surface, place the steaks on the wrap, and cover with one more piece of plastic wrap. Using the flat side of a meat pounder, pound out the steaks to a ¼-inch thickness. (If you find the plastic wrap is moving about, lightly dampen the counter with a wet rag and it will stay put perfectly.) To help tenderize the meat and to continue seasoning throughout the process, sprinkle them with a touch of salt.

After pounding the meat, allow it to rest for a few minutes, just as you allow meat to rest after cooking. It's a muscle fiber, and resting gives it a chance to relax again, which helps with rolling and the overall texture of the meat.

While the meat is resting, prep the chard. Remove the stems from the chard and roll up the leaves. Chiffonade them by cutting crosswise into very thin ribbons. (You should have about 3 cups.) Rinse in cold water and allow to dry in a strainer.

Divide the squash and leek puree between the steaks. Spread it evenly across the surface of the meat. Roll up the steaks, pulling the top flap over and down. Be careful not to squeeze out the filling but keep them tightly rolled. Secure with toothpicks, inserting one every inch or so along the roll. Alternatively, you can tie them up using butcher's twine.

COOK THE ROULADES AND CHARD

Heat a cast iron frying pan over medium-high heat and add the bacon fat. Once it is melted and hot, add the bison and sear without moving for 3 minutes. Flip the roulades over and roast in the oven for 8 minutes (this side will sear in the oven). Very carefully remove the bison from the hot pan (do not wash the pan) and place it on a cutting board to rest. Don't tent the bison with foil; it's worth what you lose in heat retention to help the muscles shrink a bit tighter around the filling, which helps the roulade stay together for slicing and presentation.

While the bison rests, place the chard in the hot pan and sprinkle with a pinch of salt. Stir gently for about 3 minutes as the chard cooks from the retained heat in the pan and the liquid released from the chard pulls the browned meat bits and bacon fat from the pan.

After the bison has rested for 5 minutes, slowly pull out the toothpicks and, with a very sharp knife, slice it into rounds about ½ inch thick. If you're concerned about the roulade staying together, you can slice it with the toothpicks still in place—just make sure you remove them all before serving. You'll only make that mistake once.

Plate a small stack of chard and a few slices of bison and garnish with thinly sliced green onions or fresh herbs.

By pan-wilting the chard in the same pan that you've browned meat in, you get a deep and complex flavor that incorporates the beautiful flavors developed in the pan. If you're pan-wilting chard and have not just cooked meat in a cast iron pan, simply heat a cast iron frying pan over high heat and add 1 tablespoon of bacon fat. Once the bacon fat is hot, remove the pan from heat, add the chard, and cook as directed.

ROASTED ACORN SQUASH WITH FRESH SAGE

SERVES 2 · COOK TIME 45 MINUTES

INGREDIENTS

1 SMALL ACORN SQUASH (JUST OVER 1 POUND), HALVED AND SEEDED

1 TABLESPOON OLIVE OIL

⅛ TEASPOON SALT

PINCH OF FRESHLY GROUND BLACK PEPPER

5 FRESH SAGE LEAVES, FOR GARNISH

Preheat the oven to 375°F.

Keeping the skin on, cut the acorn squash into 1-inch cubes. Remember to create a flat surface for cutting.

In a bowl, toss the squash with the oil, salt, and pepper. Spread the squash on a sheet pan and roast in the oven for 40 to 45 minutes, or until golden-brown and very tender. Chiffonade the sage leaves: Stack the leaves on top of the other and roll them up tightly, like a cigar, from top to bottom. Holding the "cigar" from the side and using a very sharp knife, cut the sage crosswise into very thin strips.

When the squash is done, remove it from the oven and divide it between two plates. Top with the chiffonaded sage.

ANAHEIM CHILE
AND APPLE SALAD

SERVES 4 • COOK TIME 3 TO 4 HOURS OR OVERNIGHT TO MARINATE

INGREDIENTS

2 APPLES, PREFERABLY AMBROSIA, GALA, OR FUJI, PEEL
ON AND SLICED

1 TEASPOON PLUS 1 TABLESPOON APPLE CIDER VINEGAR,
DIVIDED

3 ANAHEIM OR POBLANO CHILES, SEEDED AND CUT
INTO 3-INCH-LONG STRIPS

1 LARGE SHALLOT (2 OUNCES), SHAVED (3
TABLESPOONS)

1 TABLESPOON CHOPPED FRESH PARSLEY

2 TABLESPOONS OLIVE OIL

½ TEASPOON SALT

¼ TEASPOON FRESHLY GROUND BLACK PEPPER

Toss the sliced apples with 1 teaspoon of the vinegar.
(This will keep them from turning brown while you
prep the rest of the ingredients.)

In a bowl, mix together the apples, remaining
tablespoon of vinegar, chiles, shallot, parsley, olive oil,
salt, and pepper. Allow to marinate for at least 3 to 4
hours or overnight.

Once you cut apples they start to turn brown.
The trick to avoiding this is to dowse them
with acid—the same that's used in the recipe—
or acidulated cold water. Here, I splashed the
apples with 1 teaspoon of apple cider vinegar.
If the recipe calls for lemon instead of vinegar,
use lemon. If there is no acid in the recipe, set
the apples in cold water with a few teaspoons
of vinegar or lemon juice. The same goes for
potatoes, sunchokes, pears, avocados, and anything else that turns brown after cutting.

FLAVORS OF FALL

Fall is easily my favorite season. The leaves changing colors, the smell of woodsmoke from the first fires of the year: it's like the whole place is gently roasting. Then there's the time spent with friends and family during Thanksgiving, and of course the food. Oh, the food: rich, roasty flavors of game and fall squash combined with first-of-the-season pears or apples.

This time of year, a very good friend of mine always likes to put a big pot of water on to boil with nothing more than a few cinnamon sticks tossed in. It fills the whole house with the rich aroma of fall. This section is no boiling pot of cinnamon, but it does, with its recipes and techniques, attempt to capture the traditions and flavors of fall.

FALL

CHARD
SWEET
POTATOES BRUSSELS CAULIFLOWER
TURNIPS SPROUTS PERSIMMONS
PARSNIPS GREEN CELERY
ONIONS
MUSHROOMS
WINTER SQUASH CABBAGE
ENDIVE GREEN BEANS RADISH
SUNCHOKES
KALE

PUMPKINS

CARROTS PUMPKINS KEY LIMES
BOK CHOY DATES LIMES SORREL
BROCCOLI FIGS AVOCADOS WINTER CHARD
LETTUCE SQUASH
SHELLING BEANS GREEN BEANS
TOMATOES COLLARD GREENS
SALSIFY
RADISH

PERSIMMONS
TOMATOES BRUSSELS SPROUTS
BEETS
LETTUCE FENNEL WINTER
KALE SQUASH
ZUCCHINI TURNIPS SHELLING BEANS
MUSHROOMS
PUMPKINS

TURNIPS
FENNEL
CAULIFLOWER
MELONS
PUMPKIN
CHARD CHICORY
BROCCOLI
RUTABAGAS
PARSLEY BRUSSELS EGGPLANT
BEETS CABBAGE SPROUTS GARLIC
WINTER SQUASH
WILD MUSHROOMS
KALE CRANBERRIES
PARSNIP
CELERY

CHICORY
BRUSSELS SPROUTS
KALE PEPPERS
TOMATOES PARSNIPS
CHARD TOMATILLOS
WILD FENNEL
SUMMER MUSHROOMS
OKRA SQUASH CAULIFLOWER
BROCCOLI KOHLRABI WINTER
PUMPKINS SQUASH
RADISH
CABBAGE
ESCAROLE

COQ AU VIN

SERVES 4 • COOK TIME 2 HOURS 45 MINUTES

INGREDIENTS

1 POUND BACON, SLICED INTO MATCHSTICKS ¼ INCH BY 1 INCH

4 WHOLE CHICKEN LEGS

1 TABLESPOON PLUS 1 TEASPOON SALT, DIVIDED

2 CUPS RED WINE

6 TO 8 CUPS CHICKEN STOCK (PAGE 270), ROOM TEMPERATURE, DIVIDED

1 SMALL YELLOW ONION, JULIENNED

1 SPRIG FRESH THYME

1 BAY LEAF

3 TABLESPOONS GHEE, DIVIDED

1 POUND PEARL ONIONS, FROZEN AND PEELED

8 OUNCES BUTTON MUSHROOMS

2 BUNCHES CARROTS, PEELED

½ TEASPOON FRESHLY GROUND BLACK PEPPER

½ OUNCE UNSWEETENED CHOCOLATE

* Note: If you only make one dish in this book that is this difficult, make it this one!

PREPARE THE CHICKEN

Preheat the oven to 350°F.

Add the bacon to a large, cold braising pan or Dutch oven over medium-high heat and cook until it is nice and crispy, about 10 minutes. Using a slotted spoon, remove the bacon from the pan and set aside, keeping the rendered bacon fat in the pan.

Pat the chicken dry and lightly dust with 1 tablespoon of the salt.

Keep the pan over medium-high heat and add the chicken, skin side down. Brown for 6 to 7 minutes, or until it is golden-brown. Flip and brown the other side for another 6 to 7 minutes. Deglaze the pan with the wine and 2 cups of the stock (make sure the stock is at room temperature), using a wooden spoon to pull all the color from the bottom of the pan.

Add the yellow onion, thyme, and bay leaf. Cover and place the pan in the oven to braise for 2 hours.

COOK THE PEARL ONIONS

Melt 1 tablespoon of the ghee in a thick-bottomed sauté pan over medium heat. Add a pinch of salt and the pearl onions, and stir well. Reduce the heat to medium-low and cook for 15 minutes, or until the onions are caramelized, tossing every few minutes. You'll know they are done when they're golden-brown and just a few of them start to burn.

To save time, the onions and mushrooms can be cooked together, but the onions caramelize much better when they're cooked separately.

COOK THE MUSHROOMS

Melt 1 tablespoon of the ghee in a thick-bottomed sauté pan over medium heat. Add the mushrooms and ½ teaspoon of the salt and reduce the heat to medium-low. Cook, stirring occasionally, for 20 to 30 minutes.

COOK THE CARROTS

To slice the carrots, make one cut at a 45-degree angle across the carrot, then roll the carrot towards you by half and cut again at 45-degree angle. Continue this process, rolling the carrot back and forth.

Melt the remaining tablespoon of ghee in a thick-bottomed sauté pan over medium-high heat. Add the carrots, the remaining ½ teaspoon of salt, and 1 cup of the stock (make sure it's at room temperature). The stock should come halfway up the sides of the carrots. Stir well and continue cooking, stirring occasionally and adding the remaining stock as it reduces, for 25 minutes, or until the carrots are tender and glazed.

MAKE THE SAUCE

When the chicken has braised for 2 hours, remove it from the braising pan and transfer the braising liquid to a saucepot. Add the black pepper and reduce over high heat. Once the liquid is reduced by half, about 12 minutes, grate the unsweetened chocolate into the sauce.

To serve, spoon a serving of carrots into a bowl and place the chicken on top. Add the mushrooms, onions, and bacon, and ladle the sauce over all.

You can also place the chicken in a large pan and add the sauce, bacon, mushrooms, and pearl onions. Serve the glazed carrots on the side.

OVEN-BRAISED RIBS

SERVES 4 · COOK TIME 4 TO 5 HOURS

INGREDIENTS

2 TABLESPOONS SALT

1 TABLESPOON FRESHLY GROUND BLACK PEPPER

1 TABLESPOON GARLIC POWDER

1 TABLESPOON PAPRIKA

1 TABLESPOON DRIED BASIL

1 TEASPOON CHILI POWDER

½ TEASPOON CAYENNE PEPPER

1 RACK OF RIBS (4 TO 5 POUNDS)

1 LARGE YELLOW ONION, CHOPPED (2 CUPS)

1 POUND HEIRLOOM TOMATOES, QUARTERED

4 CUPS CHICKEN STOCK (PAGE 270)

● ●

Preheat the oven to 325°F.

In a small bowl, combine the salt, black pepper, garlic powder, paprika, dried basil, chili powder, and cayenne pepper. Massage the rib meat with the spice rub.

Add the onion and tomatoes to a roasting pan and place the ribs on top. If the whole rack doesn't fit in the pan (it probably won't), just split the ribs down the center, or even into fourths if necessary.

Pour the chicken stock over the ribs and vegetables. Cover with foil and braise for 4 to 5 hours, until the meat is falling off the bone. To serve, pour the braising liquid, onions, and tomatoes over the top of the ribs.

PORK BELLY

SERVES 6 · COOK TIME 10 HOURS, PLUS OVERNIGHT TO CHILL

This will very quickly become one of those recipes you make once or twice a month. You can serve it with pretty much any combination of veggies and it will always be awesome. It needs to be made at least one day before serving, but once cooked, it will last a week in the fridge.

You probably don't need to worry about trimming or cleaning the pork belly. If you got it from a butcher or market, it should already have been cleaned and the skin removed. You can even cook it with the skin on, but skin does have a thick, rough texture that can be weird to work with, and some find it off-putting. It's better to get it removed at the butcher, and second-best is to remove it yourself.

INGREDIENTS

FOR THE RUB

1 TABLESPOON SALT

1 TABLESPOON FRESHLY GROUND BLACK PEPPER

1 TABLESPOON DRIED OREGANO

1 TABLESPOON DRIED THYME

1 TABLESPOON DRIED MARJORAM

4 POUNDS PORK BELLY

¾ CUP HARD CIDER

½ CUP RED WINE

1 MEDIUM PINK LADY OR OTHER SWEET APPLE, THINLY SLICED

1 MEDIUM YELLOW ONION (10 OUNCES), THINLY SLICED

3 TABLESPOONS OLIVE OIL

Preheat the oven to 275°F.

In a small bowl, combine the rub ingredients. Place the pork belly, cider, wine, apple, and onion in a large, shallow baking pan and massage the rub and olive oil onto the belly. Cover the pan with a lid or aluminum foil. Place in the oven and bake for 10 hours. The pork belly will shrink a lot—expect it to be less than half its original size.

If you wish to eat the belly as-is, go right ahead. It is essentially braised pork and can be pulled and enjoyed immediately, but for our purposes here it needs to be chilled. Chilling it overnight allows it to solidify, so we can slice and sear it the next day.

Allow the belly to cool and chill overnight in the fridge. The next day, cut the belly into 1-by-3-inch pieces. Do not try to cut the belly while it is still warm; it will fall apart.

To serve, heat a large, dry cast iron frying pan over high heat, add the cut pieces to the hot, dry pan, and heat for 2 minutes on each of the four sides, until golden-brown and crispy. Serve with Chowchow (page 182) and Roasted Fall Squash (page 172), as pictured at top right, or Quick Kim Chi (page 184), as pictured at bottom right.

BEG ALICHA (STEWED LAMB WITH CARDAMOM)

SERVES 4 · COOK TIME 2½ HOURS

INGREDIENTS

FOR THE CARDAMOM PASTE

1½ TEASPOONS CARDAMOM PODS (3 PODS; SEE NOTE)

1 (1-INCH) PIECE GINGER (2 OUNCES), PEELED AND ROUGHLY CHOPPED

4 CLOVES GARLIC, ROUGHLY CHOPPED

1 TEASPOON GROUND TURMERIC

½ LEMON (OPTIONAL)

1½ TEASPOONS SALT

2 TABLESPOONS CHOPPED FRESH PARSLEY

3 TABLESPOONS OLIVE OIL

2½ POUNDS LAMB SHOULDER, TRIMMED OF EXCESS FAT AND CUBED

1 MEDIUM ONION, CUT INTO SMALL DICE

½ CUP WATER

CHOPPED FRESH PARSLEY, FOR GARNISH

This is one of three Ethiopian dishes in this book (the others are Beg Wot, page 156, and Atkilt, page 157). Ethiopian food has a very special place in my heart. If not for its amazing flavor combinations, I think I might still be the Tombstone Pizza and Old Style guy. When I worked at an Ethiopian restaurant, I learned the language from Robel and my other *winde-mehs* (Amharic for "brothers"), Yoseph, Ben-yam, and Natan, as I learned about the food from their mother, Yeshi.

Ethiopian food is spicy and makes you hot, but it's so good you keep eating. You smell the spices on your fingers the next day and remember the amazing kitfo, raw beef warmed in ghee and a chile pepper blend, or the beg alicha, so sweet and light even though it's a heavy braised lamb.

Ethiopians are an amazing people with an amazing culture. If ever there was a group of people who understand the process of cooking food, it is them. I've made some small adjust-ments to the recipes to make them Paleo-friendly, but they're really very little. Please enjoy. *Betam amasa ginalow* ("thank you very much").

* Note: The freshly ground cardamom is the highlight of this dish, so be sure to plan ahead so that you have whole cardamom pods to grind fresh. If you don't have a spice grinder, roughly chop them and tie them into cheesecloth so they are easy to remove.

Preheat the oven to 350°F.

Using a spice grinder, puree the cardamom pods until the shells are finely ground and all the seeds have been released. Transfer to a food processor and add the ginger, garlic, ground turmeric, lemon, salt, and parsley. Process to a chunky paste. Add the oil and continue to process to a mostly creamy consistency. (Don't worry about slowly adding the oil while processor is running; you can just add it and then puree.)

Put the lamb in a medium oven-safe casserole dish or Dutch oven (or other deep baking dish). Add the cardamom paste, toss to evenly coat the lamb, and mix in the diced onion. Add the water and bring to a simmer on the stovetop over medium-high heat.

Once at a simmer, cover with a lid or foil and place in the oven for 2½ hours. Top with chopped parsley to garnish.

Braising is an inherently slow process, but there is a trick to shave off a little time: bring the mixture to a simmer on the stove-top to get the meat up to temperature quickly, shortening the overall cooking time. You can place the mixture directly into the oven instead, but if you do, you will need to add 30 to 45 minutes to the cooking time.

ATKILT (SPICED VEGETABLE STEW)
(page 157)

BEG ALICHA

BEG WOT (STEWED LAMB WITH BERBERE)
(page 156)

BEG WOT (STEWED LAMB WITH BERBERE)

SERVES 4 · COOK TIME 2¾ TO 3 HOURS

This is another braising dish that would be perfect with any tough cut of meat, such as brisket. Dry cooking the onion is one of the steps that gives this dish its distinct flavor; don't skip it or think you need oil in the pan.

INGREDIENTS

1 LARGE OR 2 MEDIUM YELLOW ONIONS (1½ POUNDS), CUT INTO MEDIUM DICE

2½ TEASPOONS SALT, DIVIDED

4 TEASPOONS BERBERE, DIVIDED (SEE NOTE)

2¼ POUNDS LAMB SHOULDER, TRIMMED OF FAT AND CUBED

¼ TEASPOON FRESHLY GROUND BLACK PEPPER

⅓ CUP WATER OR CHICKEN STOCK (PAGE 270)

Preheat the oven to 350°F.

Heat a dry, medium, oven-safe casserole dish or Dutch oven (or other deep baking dish) over high heat and add the onion. Dry cook the onion for 1 to 2 minutes, then add 1 teaspoon of the salt. Cook for 2 minutes and add 1 teaspoon of the berbere. Continue to cook over high heat, stirring occasionally, until the onion starts to turn translucent. Add the lamb and reduce the heat to low. Add the remaining 3 teaspoons of berbere, the remaining 1½ teaspoons of salt, and the black pepper. Continue to cook over low heat, stirring occasionally, for 4 to 5 minutes. Add the water, raise the heat to medium-high, and bring to a simmer.

Once at a simmer, cover well with a lid or foil and place in the oven for 2½ hours. When it's done, the meat should be super tender and falling apart.

* Note: Berbere is an Ethiopian spice blend. You can find it in the organic spice section of Whole Foods, but I think the best can always be found at your local Ethiopian grocer. Just Google "Ethiopian market" and you'll find one in your town. You'll know you're in the right place when you see letters that look like this:

ወን ፡ በወንድ

They will be happy to help you and will have all the berbere you could ever need, for much, much cheaper than Whole Foods.

ATKILT (SPICED VEGETABLE STEW)

SERVES 6 · COOK TIME 40 MINUTES

Atkilt is a simple dish of cabbage, carrots, onions, and potatoes, spiced to perfection and slowly stewed. It's the African version of comfort food, really.

For this recipe, or any of the Ethiopian recipes, you can use olive oil or clarified butter. If you use clarified butter, I recommend making it half olive oil and half butter; this raises the smoke point of the butter and gives a more balanced flavor.

Heat the oil in large saucepan over medium-high heat, then add the onion, cabbage, carrots, and 2 teaspoons of the salt. Stir well, cover, and cook for 10 minutes.

Add the potatoes, the remaining 1 teaspoon of salt, the turmeric, cumin, and pepper, and stir well. Decrease the heat to medium-low and continue to cook, covered, for an additional 30 minutes, or until all vegetables are fork-tender.

INGREDIENTS

4 TABLESPOONS OLIVE OIL

1 MEDIUM YELLOW ONION (½ POUND), CUT INTO SMALL DICE

1 MEDIUM GREEN CABBAGE (1 POUND), CORED AND CUT INTO 1-INCH CUBES

4 MEDIUM CARROTS (1 POUND), CUT INTO 1-INCH ROUNDS (SEE NOTE)

3 TEASPOONS SALT, DIVIDED

1¾ POUNDS WHITE POTATOES, CUT INTO 1-INCH CUBES

2 TEASPOONS GROUND TURMERIC

1 TEASPOON GROUND CUMIN

1 TEASPOON FRESHLY GROUND BLACK PEPPER

* Note: For a slightly prettier presentation, chop the carrots like this: Make one cut at a 45-degree angle across the carrot, then roll the carrot towards you by half and cut again at 45-degree angle. Continue this process, rolling the carrot back and forth.

BRINED AND PAN-SEARED PORK CHOPS

SERVES 2 • COOK TIME 15 TO 25 MINUTES, PLUS 6 TO 12 HOURS TO BRINE

A trick to speed up brine prep time is to use as little hot water as possible—just enough to dissolve the salt and sweetener—and then add ice for the remaining water content called for in the recipe. This allows you to add the meat immediately instead of waiting hours for the brine to cool. The total brine volume should be 1 cup of brine for every 8 ounces of pork chops.

Because it is difficult to cook thick pork chops all the way through on the stovetop, I use a two-step method: first, giving them a good sear on a hot cast iron pan, and then finishing them in the oven.

INGREDIENTS

FOR THE BRINE

2 CUPS WATER

2 TABLESPOONS SALT

1 TABLESPOON WHOLE BLACK PEPPERCORNS

2 TABLESPOONS APPLE CIDER VINEGAR

2 CLOVES GARLIC, SMASHED

½ SPRIG ROSEMARY, OR ANY FRESH HERB

2 TABLESPOONS HONEY (OPTIONAL; SEE NOTE)

4 CUPS ICE

2 (1-INCH-THICK) PORK CHOPS

2 TABLESPOONS AVOCADO OIL

In a medium saucepan over high heat, bring all ingredients for the brine, except the ice, to a rapid boil and continue to boil for 7 minutes.

Pour the hot brine mixture into a large heatproof bowl and add the ice. Submerge the pork chops in the brine, place in the refrigerator, and allow to brine for 6 to 12 hours.

Remove the pork chops from the brine, pat completely dry with paper towels, and discard the brining liquid.

Preheat the oven to 400°F. Have a sheet pan ready for the chops.

Heat a 12-inch cast iron frying pan over high heat and, once the pan is hot, add the avocado oil. Right when the oil starts to smoke, add the pork chops.

Start by holding the chops upright with tongs so that the fat cap is facing down in the pan. Once the fat is rendered and crispy, roll over to the first side. Let sear for 3 minutes, then flip over to other side. Cook for 3 to 4 minutes until good and golden-brown, then place the chops on a sheet pan. Finish in the oven for no more than 6 minutes for medium doneness. If you like pork cooked all the way through, bake the chops for a total of 9 to 12 minutes. Let them rest for 5 minutes once they're removed from oven before slicing or serving. Serve with Cauliflower Dumplings (page 164) or Pumpkin Dumplings (page 165).

* Note: Before pouring honey into the measuring spoon, add a drop of oil to the spoon and rub it on the inside surface. The honey will easily glide out of the spoon, giving you more accurate measuring and no waste.

SPAGHETTI SQUASH MEXICANA

SERVES 2 AS AN ENTRÉE OR 4 AS A SIDE • COOK TIME 40 MINUTES

INGREDIENTS

1 SPAGHETTI SQUASH

1 TEASPOON SALT, PLUS MORE TO TASTE

1 TABLESPOON OLIVE OIL

2 TEASPOONS GROUND CUMIN

½ CUP TOASTED PEPITAS

1 TABLESPOON GHEE

FRESHLY GROUND BLACK PEPPER

Preheat the oven to 350°F.

Slice off the top and bottom of squash to give yourself a flat surface to work with, then cut it in half from top bottom. Scoop out the seeds and pulp from the center and discard. Place the squash face up on a large piece of aluminum foil and lightly sprinkle with the salt and oil. Wrap the squash tightly in the aluminum foil and place in the oven for 40 minutes.

Remove from the oven and let sit for 10 minutes, or until it's cooled enough to handle. Scoop out the flesh and toss it with the cumin, toasted pepitas, and ghee. Season with salt and pepper to taste.

MUSHROOM RAGOUT WITH GREMOLATA

SERVES 4 • COOK TIME 30 MINUTES

Any combination of mushrooms will work in this rich, earthy dish—king oyster, shiitake, maitake, beech, hedgehog, yellow foot chanterelles, black trumpet, enoki, and so on. Just make sure you allow each kind of mushroom the right cook time.

Gremolata is a classic condiment that combines citrus, garlic, and parsley. It goes well with hearty lamb, oysters, and, as here, earthy mushrooms.

INGREDIENTS

3 TABLESPOONS GHEE, DIVIDED

1 POUND MIXED MUSHROOMS

SALT, ADDED A PINCH AT A TIME THROUGHOUT THE COOKING PROCESS

1 CUP CHICKEN STOCK AT ROOM TEMPERTURE (PAGE 270), DIVIDED

FOR THE GREMOLATA

½ TEASPOON FINELY MINCED GARLIC

½ CUP MINCED KUMQUAT

¾ CUP FINELY CHOPPED FRESH PARSLEY

¼ TEASPOON SALT

Heat 1 tablespoon of the ghee in a thick-bottomed sauté pan over medium heat. Add the wettest and thickest mushrooms first, sprinkle with salt, and cook for a few minutes. Add the remaining mushrooms and 1 tablespoon of the ghee, and sprinkle with salt. Continue to cook until the mushrooms start to become tender and brown, about 6 minutes, then add the remaining tablespoon of ghee and sprinkle with salt.

Cook for a few minutes and then add ½ cup of the stock (make sure it's at room temperature) to pull the color from the pan. Continue to cook and caramelize the mushrooms for another 10 minutes or so, adding the remaining ½ cup of stock to deglaze the pan. Once the mushrooms are very tender and have a rich glaze, they're done.

In a medium bowl, combine all the ingredients for the gremolata and mix well. Sprinkle on the mushroom ragout and serve.

CAULIFLOWER DUMPLINGS

SERVES 4 · COOK TIME 45 MINUTES

These and the Pumpkin Dumplings (page 165) can be made ahead of time, frozen, and reheated before serving. The two kinds of dumplings offer a good contrast in texture and density when served together, and they're great with Brined and Pan-Seared Pork Chops (page 158).

INGREDIENTS

AVOCADO OR OLIVE OIL, FOR GREASING THE PAN

2 MEDIUM HEADS CAULIFLOWER (3 POUNDS TOTAL)

4 LARGE EGGS

⅔ TEASPOON SALT

¼ TEASPOON FRESHLY GROUND BLACK PEPPER

Preheat the oven to 325°F. Grease 12 muffin cups or 8 ornamental baking molds.

Remove the stem and the leaves from the cauliflower and discard. Using a paring knife, cut the cauliflower into medium florets and remove any remaining stems.

Place the florets in a fine-mesh strainer and steam until soft, 10 to 12 minutes. (If you do not have a fine-mesh strainer, you can use a steamer basket.) Allow the steamed cauliflower to cool and transfer it to a food processor. Pulse in the processor until you have a fine texture.

Add the eggs, salt, and pepper to the processor and process for 3 minutes, or until you have a smooth batter.

Fill each prepared muffin cup to just short of the top—the mixture will not rise—and place in the oven for 30 minutes, testing after 25 minutes. Test the mixture by sticking a knife in the middle; if the knife comes out clean, they are done.

To store in the freezer, first cool on a sheet pan lined with wax paper. Freeze the dumplings on the pan and then, once frozen, store in a freezer bag for up to 2 months. Reheat by placing on oiled sheet pan and heating in a 350°F oven for 10 to 13 minutes.

PUMPKIN DUMPLINGS

SERVES 4 • COOK TIME 2 HOURS

INGREDIENTS

AVOCADO OR OLIVE OIL, FOR GREASING THE PANS

1 (1½-POUND) SUGAR PUMPKIN OR OTHER WINTER SQUASH

32 GRAMS ARROWROOT POWDER (1 OUNCE; SEE NOTE)

240 GRAMS ALMOND FLOUR (8 OUNCES; SEE NOTE)

1⅓ TEASPOONS SALT

⅛ TEASPOON FRESHLY GROUND BLACK PEPPER

4 LARGE EGG YOLKS

*Note: To really execute this dish perfectly, use the weight, not volume, measurements. The moisture content of the dumplings requires precise measuring that's best obtained with a kitchen scale.

That being said, if you don't have a kitchen scale, you can use 1/4 cup arrowroot powder and 1 2/3 cups almond flour. The consistency may not be exactly what it should, but it'll still taste good.

Preheat the oven to 325°F. Grease 12 standard muffin cups.

Cut off the very top and bottom of the sugar pumpkin, cut in half from top to bottom, seed, and place in a roasting pan, open side down, with a little water. Cover and steam-roast until done, about 50 to 60 minutes. Remove from the oven, place in a dry baking pan, and return to oven. Roast, uncovered, for 20 minutes to dry the pumpkin out. (This step is important; without it, the dumplings will be too wet and won't hold together.) Allow the pumpkin to cool and then puree in a food processor. You should have 1½ to 2 cups of puree.

In a mixing bowl, combine the pumpkin puree, arrowroot powder, almond flour, salt, pepper, and egg yolks.

Fill each prepared muffin cup to just short of the top—the mixture will not rise—and place in the oven for 30 minutes, testing after 25 minutes. Test the mixture by sticking a knife in the middle; if the knife comes out clean, they are done.

To store in the freezer, first cool on a sheet pan lined with wax paper. Freeze the dumplings on a pan and then, once frozen, store in a freezer bag for up to 2 months. Reheat by placing on oiled sheet pan and heating in a 350°F oven for 10 to 13 minutes.

ROMANESCO AND SWEET POTATOES

SERVES 4 · COOK TIME 35 MINUTES

When working with romanesco, cut with care and go over it a few times—just a little extra work yields amazing results. It's best to cut it in a way that gets you the desired bite-sized pieces while retaining the natural beauty of the vegetable. This is done with a small paring knife and time. Using just the tip of the knife, cut off whole pieces of the romanesco and work from large to small, breaking it down to bite-sized pieces.

INGREDIENTS

1 HEAD ROMANESCO, CUT INTO SMALL FLORETS (ABOUT 2 CUPS)

1 TABLESPOON OLIVE OIL

¼ TEASPOON SALT

1 POUND PURPLE SWEET POTATOES, CUT INTO MEDIUM DICE

1 TABLESPOON GHEE

2 TABLESPOONS CHOPPED SHALLOTS

½ CUP CHICKEN STOCK (PAGE 270)

Preheat the oven to 400°F.

Blanch the romanesco for 3 minutes, dip it in an ice bath, and dry it in a colander. Lightly coat it with the olive oil and salt and place it on a sheet pan. Roast for 15 minutes—the romanesco will soften, but it will not start to turn golden-brown.

Blanch the sweet potatoes for 3 minutes, place in ice water for 2 to 3 minutes, and drain. They should be just shy of tender enough to eat. If you cut the potatoes into larger pieces, they'll need to cook a bit longer.

Heat the ghee in a large, thick-bottomed sauté pan over medium heat. Once the ghee is hot, add the shallots and sauté for 1 minute, then add the romaesco and sweet potatoes and sauté until tender, approximately 6 to 7 minutes. While you sauté the vegetables, bring the stock to a simmer in a saucepan. As soon as you start to see some color and the vegetables are sticking to the bottom of the pan, add the simmering stock to the sauté pan. This will release the vegetables and the fond from the bottom of the pan.

Blanching not only makes vegetables cook faster, it also helps their colors stay vibrant, keeps them moist during oven roasting, and helps them brown better in a sauté pan. It's perfect when you are cooking for a dinner party, since it lets you do most of the cooking in advance. After blanching, quickly roast or sear the vegetables before you put them on the plate.

CHIVE MASHED POTATOES

SERVES 6 • COOK TIME 35 MINUTES

INGREDIENTS

3 TABLESPOONS SALT, DIVIDED

3 POUNDS YUKON GOLD POTATOES, QUARTERED

1 CUP HEAVY WHIPPING CREAM (SEE NOTE)

2 TABLESPOONS GHEE

¼ CUP ROUGHLY CHOPPED CHIVES

●

Fill a large stockpot with water and add 2 tablespoons of the salt. Place the stockpot over high heat and, when the water is at a rolling boil, add the potatoes. Boil until the potatoes are fork-tender, approximately 20 to 25 minutes.

Drain all the water from the potatoes. Add the whipping cream, ghee, and the remaining tablespoon of salt, and mash and whip the potatoes with a stiff whisk to a smooth texture. Fold in the chives and serve.

* Note: If you don't want to use whipping cream, you can substitute an equal amount of rich, roasted, and reduced chicken stock.

ROASTED FALL SQUASH

In this recipe the squash is roasted at two temperatures: the lower temp allows the vegetable to soften and stay moist, while the higher temp helps with browning. This keeps the veggies moist on the inside and crunchy on the outside, without making them chewy. It's a great trick for cooking any root vegetable.

Preheat the oven to 350°F.

In a large bowl, combine all the ingredients, then spread evenly onto a sheet pan. Bake for 30 minutes, give the veg a stir with a wooden spoon, and then raise the oven temperature to 400°F and bake for an additional 30 minutes.

INGREDIENTS

2 SUGAR PUMPKINS OR CARNIVAL SQUASH (1 POUND TOTAL), SKIN ON, SEEDED AND CHOPPED (2 TO 3 CUPS)

1 APPLE, PEEL ON AND CUT INTO MEDIUM DICE (1 CUP)

2 TABLESPOONS OLIVE OIL

1 TEASPOON DRIED SAVORY

½ TEASPOON SALT

¼ TEASPOON FRESHLY GROUND BLACK PEPPER

ROASTED BUTTERNUT SQUASH WITH CURRANTS

SERVES 6 • COOK TIME 35 MINUTES

This side dish is perfect around the holidays. I love it because it's almost as sweet as a dessert but there is no sugar added; it's just naturally sweet from roasting. An added benefit: This recipe gives you a reason to roast up a pan of pumpkin seeds. I usually make more than what this recipe calls for to have the extra around for a nice snack.

INGREDIENTS

1 MEDIUM BUTTERNUT SQUASH (ABOUT 2¾ POUNDS; SEE NOTES)

¾ TEASPOON SALT, DIVIDED

½ TEASPOON FRESHLY GROUND BLACK PEPPER, DIVIDED

3 TABLESPOONS OLIVE OIL

2 TABLESPOONS RAW PUMPKIN SEEDS (SEE NOTES)

¼ TEASPOON GROUND CINNAMON

¼ TEASPOON GROUND STAR ANISE

2 TABLESPOONS CURRANTS (SEE NOTES)

Preheat the oven to 350°F. Have two oven racks in place.

Cut off the very top and the very bottom of the butternut squash. Scoop out the seeds, then peel each half. Cut into ½-inch cubes and toss with ¼ teaspoon of the salt, ¼ teaspoon of the black pepper, and the oil.

Lay out on a sheet pan and roast for 35 minutes, stirring halfway through.

At the same time, spread the pumpkin seeds on a sheet pan and bake for 25 to 35 minutes, stirring once halfway through, until the seeds take on a nice toasted, golden-brown color.

Halfway through cooking, switch the rack positions of the squash and pumpkin seeds, so everything cooks evenly.

Toss the roasted butternut squash with the remaining ½ teaspoon of salt and ¼ teaspoon of black pepper, along with the cinnamon, star anise, and currants. Top with the roasted pumpkin seeds.

* Notes: If your squash is larger or smaller, just adjust the ingredients as needed. It's great practice.

I usually roast the pumpkin seeds at the same time as the squash, but they can be done ahead of time. If you are roasting the seeds alone, I recommend roasting them at 325°F for 30 to 40 minutes.

We use currants for this recipe, but you can substitute dried blueberries or cranberries. Remember to make sure they are unsweetened.

ROASTED SPAGHETTI SQUASH

SERVES 6 • COOK TIME 1 HOUR 15 MINUTES

INGREDIENTS

1 MEDIUM SPAGHETTI SQUASH (ABOUT 2 POUNDS)

1 TEASPOON OLIVE OIL

¼ TEASPOON SALT

⅛ TEASPOON FRESHLY GROUND BLACK PEPPER

●

Preheat the oven to 400°F.

Slice off the top and the bottom the squash—this will also give you a flat cutting surface. Slice the spaghetti squash in half lengthwise from top to bottom. Remove the seeds. Using your hands, coat the inside with the oil, salt, and pepper. Place open side down on a sheet pan, cover with aluminum foil, and bake for 1 hour 15 minutes.

The squash should be tender to the touch. Allow to cool for 5 minutes, then, using a fork, scrape out the inside. It will easily shred into strands of "spaghetti."

Before serving, you may want to lightly coat the squash with a touch of olive oil or ghee, salt, and pepper. Or serve it with Burst Tomato Sauce (page 108).

You'll notice that this is a fall dish that can be served with a summer tomato sauce. Summer and fall produce tend to overlap in August and September, when you'll find both tomatoes and early fall squash. Even so, canning and freezing are great ways to preserve the sauces that you make with fresh ingredients in peak season, so you can use them throughout the year.

SAUTÉED BLACK TRUMPET MUSHROOMS

SERVES 4 • COOK TIME 5 MINUTES, PLUS 1 HOUR 15 MINUTES TO ROAST SPAGHETTI SQUASH

Black trumpets have a really earthy, deep, umami flavor that makes them worth searching out. If you can't find them, you can substitute maitake or brown beech mushrooms. The "don't ever wash mushrooms" rule doesn't apply here. With the black trumpet, you really need to clean them. I walk you through the process in the instructions.

INGREDIENTS

1 CUP BLACK TRUMPET MUSHROOMS (2 OUNCES)

1 TABLESPOON GHEE

PINCH OF SALT

1 CUP ARUGULA (3 OUNCES)

2 CUPS ROASTED SPAGHETTI SQUASH (PAGE 176)

Set up three small bowls with ice water. Plunge the mushrooms into the first bowl and shake them all around to wash, lift them out, and place them into the second bowl. Repeat the process and then do the same in the third bowl. Place the mushrooms in a colander and let dry. Check them over for twigs, dirt, leaves, and spiders. (Yeah, spiders.) Then repeat the washing process one more time. Drain and lay out on paper towels to dry.

Once the mushrooms are completely dry, heat a sauté pan over high heat. Add the ghee and let it go until it is really hot, about 2 minutes. Add the mushrooms and a sprinkle of salt and sauté, tossing every 30 seconds, for about 2 minutes. Fold in the arugula and spaghetti squash; cook for about 1 minute, stirring continuously; and serve.

CHICKEN PHO

SERVES 4 • COOK TIME 8 MINUTES, PLUS 30 MINUTES TO MAKE THE PHO BROTH

This recipe is great for using leftover chicken, or any pulled meat for that matter. I really like the Beer Butt Chicken (page 96) for this, but any braised or roasted pulled chicken will do.

Pho is a dish built for interpretation. You can use different vegetables; just remember that the denser or larger the vegetable, the longer the poaching time. Pho is amazing with a poached egg (page 132), some kim chi (page 184), roasted pork belly (page 152), sliced radish. Have fun with it and don't be afraid to make it your own.

In a stockpot, bring the prepared pho broth to a simmer over medium-high heat. Once at a simmer, reduce the heat to medium or medium-low to maintain a gentle simmer.

Add the carrots and mushrooms to the broth and poach for 4 minutes—just until they are cooked through. Add the chard, stir well, and remove the pan from the heat.

Divide the chicken among four serving bowls. Pour the soup over the chicken. Garnish with the sliced jalapeños, cilantro leaves, and green onions. It's also borderline mandatory to add a squeeze of fresh lime.

INGREDIENTS

1 RECIPE PHO BROTH (PAGE 276)

1 CUP PEELED AND THINLY SLICED CARROTS

1 CUP QUARTERED BUTTON MUSHROOMS

2 CUPS STEMMED AND CHIFFONADED SWISS CHARD (½ BUNCH)

1½ POUNDS PULLED CHICKEN

2 SMALL JALAPEÑO PEPPERS, THINLY SLICED (SEEDED IF YOU DON'T WANT TOO MUCH SPICE), FOR GARNISH

¼ CUP FRESH CILANTRO LEAVES, FOR GARNISH

2 TABLESPOONS THINLY SLICED GREEN ONION OR CHIVES, FOR GARNISH

1 LIME, SLICED INTO WEDGES, FOR GARNISH

CHOWCHOW

YIELD ABOUT 1 QUART · COOK TIME 30 MINUTES

Chowchow usually has green tomatoes; mine doesn't. I don't like the grittiness of the seeds, and since the only reason to add the tomatoes is for the tartness, I skip them and add apple cider vinegar instead.

Chowchow can be used anytime you would use relish. It's awesome in salads, a perfect topping for pork belly (page 152), and excellent tossed with pulled chicken (page 90). A dollop of sunchoke puree, a perfectly seared scallop, and a spoonful of chowchow for a first-course plate will wow your dinner guests. Have fun with it; it's delicious.

Heat the oil in a medium saucepan over medium-high heat, then add the onion, cabbage, and salt and cook for 3 minutes. Add the chopped garlic and cook for 3 minutes. Add the bell peppers, lower the heat to medium, and cook for 3 minutes. Add the vinegar, honey, turmeric, and black pepper and continue to cook for 20 minutes. Cool to room temperature and store in a glass mason jar in the fridge for up to 2 weeks.

INGREDIENTS

2 TABLESPOONS OLIVE OIL

1½ CUPS CHOPPED YELLOW ONION

1 CUP CORED AND CHOPPED GREEN CABBAGE

1½ TEASPOONS SALT

2 TABLESPOONS CHOPPED GARLIC

2 CUPS FINELY DICED BELL PEPPERS (ANY COLOR OR COMBINATION)

¼ CUP APPLE CIDER VINEGAR

2 TABLESPOONS HONEY

¼ TEASPOON GROUND TURMERIC

¼ TEASPOON FRESHLY GROUND BLACK PEPPER

QUICK KIM CHI

YIELD 2 QUARTS · COOK TIME 10 MINUTES

Pouring boiling liquid brine over vegetables, as this recipe calls for, creates a
quick, faux kim chi. This is by no means
authentic Korean kim chi, which involves
fermenting the vegetables for a long, long
time, traditionally in clay pots buried in
the ground. This short-cut method does
produce similar flavor profiles, though.
Jill Ciciarelli's book *Fermented* has a
great how-to on the real deal.

INGREDIENTS

FOR THE QUICK PICKLING BRINE

1 CUP APPLE CIDER VINEGAR

1 CUP WATER

1 TEASPOON SEVEN-SPICE BLEND

1 TABLESPOON OLIVE OIL

1 CUP SLICED YELLOW ONION

2 CUPS CORED AND SLICED GREEN CABBAGE

1 CUP CORED AND SLICED RED CABBAGE

1½ TEASPOONS SALT, DIVIDED

2 TABLESPOONS CHOPPED JALAPEÑO PEPPER (SEEDED
FOR LESS HEAT IF DESIRED)

1 TABLESPOON SLICED GARLIC

2 CUPS MEDIUM-DICED MIXED BELL PEPPERS

● ●

You will need two saucepans for this recipe.

In one small saucepan, bring the vinegar, water, and
seven-spice blend to a boil over high heat.

While the first saucepan heats, in a second, large
saucepan, heat the oil over medium heat and add the
onion, green and red cabbage, and ½ teaspoon of the
salt; cook for 2 minutes. Add the jalapeño and garlic
and cook for 2 minutes. Add the mixed peppers and the
remaining 1 teaspoon of salt; cook for 2 minutes.

By this time the liquid in the first pan should be at a
boil. Pour the boiling pickling brine into the saucepan
with the vegetables and immediately remove from the
heat.

Let the mixture cool, place in glass jars, and store in the
fridge overnight before using.

CHOCOLATE PUMPKIN SEEDS

YIELD 3 CUPS · COOK TIME 35 TO 40 MINUTES

INGREDIENTS

3 CUPS FRESH PUMPKIN SEEDS

2 TABLESPOONS OLIVE OIL

PINCH OF SALT

FOR THE CHOCOLATE COATING

½ CUP HONEY

⅓ CUP RAW CACAO POWDER

1 TEASPOON CINNAMON

½ TEASPOON SALT

½ TEASPOON VANILLA EXTRACT

Rinse the seeds in a colander under running water, then spread them evenly on a sheet pan and allow to dry overnight.

Preheat the oven to 325°F.

Toss the pumpkin seeds in the olive oil and salt and roast for 25 minutes. Remove from the oven and allow to cool for 10 minutes.

In a medium bowl, whisk together the ingredients for the chocolate coating. Pour the chocolate mixture over the cooled seeds. Use your hands to evenly coat the seeds with the mixture—wear gloves or lightly coat your hands with olive oil to keep the coating from sticking to your hands.

Bake in the oven for 10 to 15 minutes. The seeds should be light golden-brown and crispy. Allow to cool completely before serving.

COCONUT CURRY PUMPKIN SEEDS

YIELD 3 CUPS • COOK TIME 30 TO 40 MINUTES

INGREDIENTS

3 CUPS FRESH PUMPKIN SEEDS

½ CUP MELTED COCONUT OIL

1 TABLESPOON COCONUT FLAKES

½ TABLESPOON CURRY POWDER

1 TEASPOON SALT

Rinse the seeds in a colander under running water, then spread them evenly on a sheet pan and allow to dry overnight.

Preheat the oven to 325°F.

In a small bowl, combine the coconut oil, coconut flakes, curry powder, and salt, and mix well. Add the seeds and toss to coat evenly.

Spread the seeds on a sheet pan and roast for 30 to 40 minutes, until golden-brown and crunchy. Allow to cool completely before serving.

CHOCOLATE PUMPKIN PIE

MAKES 1 PIE • COOK TIME 1 HOUR 40 MINUTES

INGREDIENTS

1 (1-POUND) PUMPKIN, ANY VARIETY (SEE NOTE)

¼ RAW CACAO POWDER

½ CUP COCONUT FLOUR

1 TEASPOON BAKING SODA

1 TEASPOON SALT

¼ CUP MELTED COCONUT OIL

½ TEASPOON VANILLA EXTRACT

½ CUP RAW HONEY

6 EGGS

FOR THE FROSTING

2 CUPS HEAVY WHIPPING CREAM

1 TEASPOON CINNAMON

2 TABLESPOONS HONEY

* Note: Okay, yes, you can use canned pumpkin here, but there are a couple things you should know: First, it's not really pumpkin. Most canned pumpkin is really squash. Second, it's not that hard to use real pumpkin. Give it a shot.

Preheat the oven to 375˚F.

Split the pumpkin and scoop out the seeds. Place each half in a baking pan, fill each pumpkin half halfway with water, cover with foil, and bake for 45 minutes. Let cool for about 20 minutes and then pour out the water. Then, using a dish towel to hold the pumpkin, scoop out the flesh and let it come to room temperature.

Place the pumpkin flesh in the bowl of a stand mixer and mix on low for a few minutes. Add the cacao powder, coconut flour, baking soda, and salt while the mixer is on. Pause and add the coconut oil, vanilla, and honey. Return the mixer to low and add one egg at a time.

Continue mixing on low till it's emulsified, about 1 minute. Stop and scrape the sides of the bowl with a spoon, then mix for 10 more seconds. Lightly coat a 9-inch springform pan with coconut oil and pour in the mixture.

Bake for 40 to 55 minutes, or until a knife inserted into the middle comes out clean.

Run a butter knife along the inside of the pan to release it and allow to cool for 1 hour.

While the cake cools, make the frosting: Place the heavy cream in the bowl of a stand mixer. Using the whisk attachment, whip on high till you have soft peaks. Add the cinnamon and slowly drizzle in the room-temperature honey while whipping. Don't overbeat: look for the peaks and then stop.

Frost the cake with the whipped cream mixture or serve a dollop on the side.

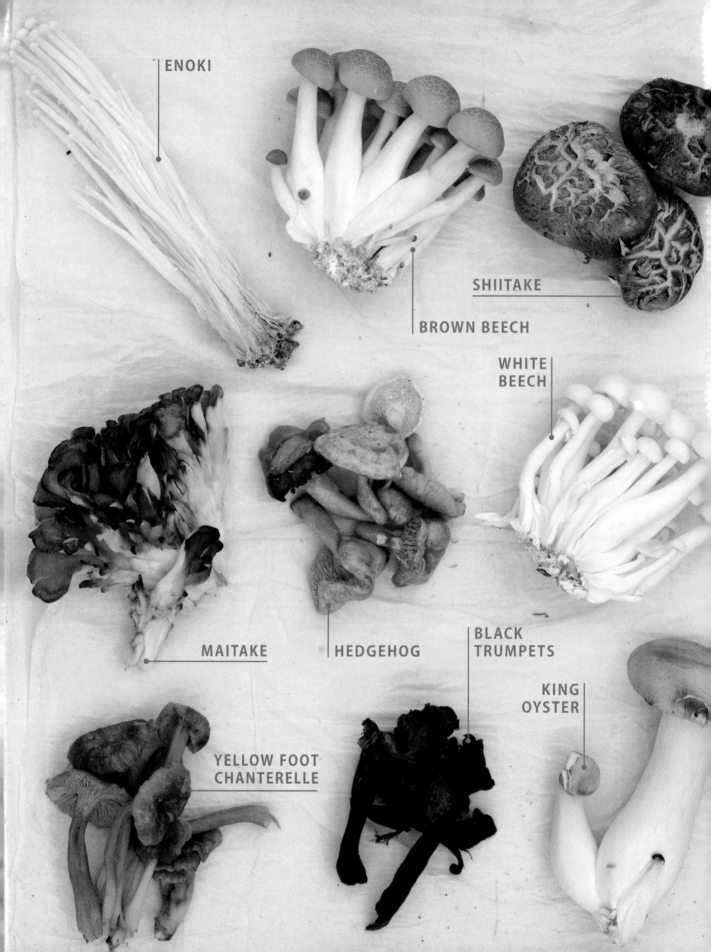

ENOKI

BROWN BEECH

SHIITAKE

WHITE
BEECH

MAITAKE

HEDGEHOG

BLACK
TRUMPETS

KING
OYSTER

YELLOW FOOT
CHANTERELLE

GUIDE TO MUSHROOMS

ENOKI
These cook super fast and are a great addition to almost any soup. With Paleo soups in particular, where you don't have traditional noodles as an option, they can add a noodle-like texture, along with a soft, roasted flavor.

BROWN BEECH
These break apart into perfect little mushrooms, ideal for pan roasting and serving with other vegetables. They keep their texture even with thorough roasting and have a super nutty flavor.

SHIITAKE
These are great for just about any use you could think of. They're perfect for soups or sautés; just be sure never to use the stems for anything. They are not edible.

MAITAKE
(Hen of the Woods)
I'd be hard-pressed to pick a mushroom I like better than this guy. It has a serious, meaty taste, rich and earthy. Plus, the bottoms, which come off, make the best mushroom stock. Just steep them in water for 30 minutes at a low simmer—done.

HEDGEHOG
A lighter version of a chanterelle, they are named for the little teeth that come out from the bottom, but don't be fooled: they are very delicate. When sautéed in ghee, they remind me of roasted hazelnuts.

WHITE BEECH
The white version of the brown beech mushroom, these don't have as much flavor on their own, but I've fallen in love with the flavors they absorb with quick pickling or smoking. They're a perfect flavor vessel and have a great texture.

YELLOW FOOT CHANTERELLE
With an almost smoky taste, these mushrooms bring a lot to the party. They can be featured on their own or be the star with simple vegetables like turnips.

BLACK TRUMPETS
These are a horrible pain to clean but well worth the effort. They're dense, nutty, and earthy—like putting a walk through the Northwest on your plate. They're great with fatty fish like black cod.

KING OYSTER
(King Trumpet)
The "king" in the name refers to how big they are. The stems make up most of the mushroom, which means a long cooking time, so stews and braising bring out the best in this mushroom.

FLAVORS OF WINTER

Winter is like the redheaded stepchild of seasons. It immediately brings to mind bland, earth-colored tubers and tough cuts of meat that are cooked for hours and always result in heavy dishes. Sure, this is true enough, but it's not necessarily a bad thing. Brisket braised all day with new potatoes and carrots is absolutely the perfect thing to eat after shoveling a driveway.

Winter is also, however, the season of bright, sugary beets and fresh, clean citrus. A shaved beet, fennel, and blood orange salad is one of the most colorful things you can put on a plate, and it's in season in January. In this section you will find some delicious, unexpected meals while learning about techniques, ingredients, and flavor profiles you may not have associated with winter.

WINTER

FENNEL CELERY CABBAGE
SPINACH SUNCHOKES
TURNIPS BRUSSELS SPROUTS
MUSTARD WINTER SQUASH
GREENS PARSNIP ENDIVE
COLLARD GREENS BOK CHOY
SWEET POTATOES CAULIFLOWER
ARUGULA
KALE

LEMONS
AVOCADOS  RUTABAGAS CARROTS
RADISH BRUSSELS SPROUTS
CELERY SWEET POTATOES CELERY ROOT LETTUCE
COLLARD GREENS PARSNIP BROCCOLI RABE
KOHLRABI LEEKS CAULIFLOWER BOK CHOY
KALE CABBAGE SORREL
BROCCOLI
GARLIC
CHARD

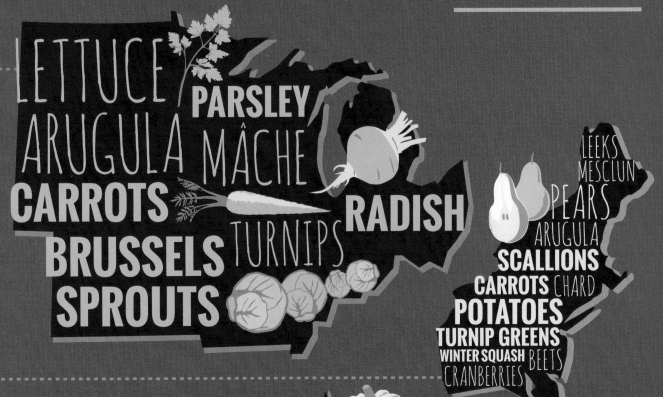

LETTUCE
PARSLEY
ARUGULA
MÂCHE
CARROTS
RADISH
TURNIPS
BRUSSELS
SPROUTS

LEEKS
MESCLUN
PEARS
ARUGULA
SCALLIONS
CARROTS CHARD
POTATOES
TURNIP GREENS
WINTER SQUASH BEETS
CRANBERRIES

WINTER
SQUASH
CARROTS
CHICORY TOMATOES SPINACH
PEPPERS
CABBAGE
RADISH
FAVA
PARSNIPS
BEANS
BRUSSELS SPROUTS TOMATILLOS
BROCCOLI
FENNEL
CHARD

BRAISED LAMB

SERVES 9 · YIELD ABOUT 10 CUPS · COOK TIME 3 HOURS

This delicious braised lamb is great on its own, and the leftovers can be used in a number of recipes: Lamb Scramble (page 200), Braised Lamb and Kale Salad (page 244), and Lamb Quenelles (page 202). But it's also your basic braising recipe for just about any tough cut of meat, such as pork shoulder, brisket, or boar shank. It's made with basic flavors that are melded together over a long period with low heat, making it easy, simple, and the perfect base for so many recipes.

INGREDIENTS

WHOLE LEG OF LAMB (4 TO 5 POUNDS)

2 TEASPOONS SALT, PLUS ADDITIONAL FOR DUSTING THE SHANK

1 TEASPOON FRESHLY GROUND BLACK PEPPER

2 CUPS DRY WHITE WINE, SUCH AS SAUVIGNON BLANC

2 YELLOW ONIONS, THINLY SLICED (ABOUT 2 CUPS)

2 TO 3 SPRIGS FRESH THYME

3 CUPS CHICKEN STOCK (PAGE 270)

Preheat the oven to 375°F.

Heat a dry large braising pan (ceramic-coated cast iron pan, thick-bottomed Dutch oven, or thick-bottomed soup pot with oven-safe lid) over high heat. Dust the lamb shank with salt and the pepper. Once the pan is super hot, add the lamb, skin side down.

Sear for a total of 6 to 10 minutes; start checking the color at 6 minutes. When it begins to turn a deep golden-brown, add the wine, onions, and thyme. Once the meat has browned, after about 6 more minutes, carefully pull the shank and fond from the bottom of the pan. Reduce for 10 minutes, then add the stock and the 2 teaspoons of salt and reduce for 5 more minutes. Cover and place in the oven.

Cook for 2 to 2½ hours. Allow to cool for 30 minutes, then pull the meat from the bones. Reserve the bones for stock.

LAMB SCRAMBLE

SERVES 2 · COOK TIME 20 MINUTES, PLUS 3 HOURS TO BRAISE THE LAMB

INGREDIENTS

2 TABLESPOONS GHEE, DIVIDED

1 CUP SHAVED SHALLOTS

3 PINCHES OF SALT, DIVIDED

1½ CUPS PEELED AND DICED EGGPLANT

4 EGGS

PINCH OF FRESHLY GROUND BLACK PEPPER

1½ CUPS BRAISED LAMB (PAGE 198)

1 TEASPOON ROUGHLY CHOPPED FRESH ROSEMARY

1 CUP BABY ARUGULA, PLUS ADDITIONAL FOR GARNISH

There is a lot of water in the eggplant, and you want it to cook out for the purposes of this dish.

Heat 1 tablespoon of the ghee in a large skillet over medium-high heat. Add the shallots and a pinch of the salt, and stir well. Cook for 3 minutes, or until the shallots lightly brown and become slightly translucent. Add the eggplant, a pinch of the salt, and ½ tablespoon of the ghee, and stir well. Cook for 5 minutes, stirring occasionally, then add the remaining ½ tablespoon of ghee. Cook for another 5 minutes, or until the eggplant has softened and is golden-brown.

While the eggplant mixture cooks, whisk the eggs in a small bowl and add the remaining pinch of salt and the pepper. Set aside.

Add the lamb to the eggplant mixture, reduce the heat to low, and fold in the rosemary. After everything is mixed, bring the heat back up to medium-high. Once the pan is hot, push the eggplant mixture to the side and use the other half of the pan to cook the eggs.

Add the eggs to the pan. Once they begin to cook, add the arugula and scramble it with the eggs. Mix together the eggs and eggplant mixture to finish. Garnish with fresh arugula.

LAMB QUENELLES

SERVES 4 • COOK TIME 30 MINUTES, PLUS 3 HOURS TO BRAISE THE LAMB

INGREDIENTS

4 CUPS BRAISED LAMB (PAGE 198), WARM

2 TABLESPOONS CHOPPED FRESH PARSLEY

½ CUP SHELLED PISTACHIOS, RAW AND UNSALTED

¼ CUP BACON FAT OR ANY RENDERED ANIMAL FAT, MELTED

1 LARGE EGG

SALT

OLIVE OR AVOCADO OIL, FOR FRYING (THE EXACT AMOUNT DEPENDS ON THE PAN)

FOR THE BATTER

1 LARGE EGG

2 TABLESPOONS WATER

1 CUP ALMOND FLOUR

"Quenelles" traditionally refers to the method of making a mixture into football-like shapes using two spoons (or just one for the real pros) and then poaching them. In this recipe, we make a quenelle shape but fry them like croquettes. Very tasty. Lamb quenelles are great served with Celeriac Puree (page 218), Roasted Beets with Salsify and Fennel Fronds (page 220), and Oil-Poached Salsify (page 222), or as a snack with Chimichurri Sauce (page 252) or a puree of squash soup.

When you get a technique like making quenelles down, you'll soon learn that you can do one thing thirty different ways, and this is a perfect example. Anytime you have leftover braised meat and you are going to have a dinner party, use this recipe to blow your guests' minds. You can use this same recipe with confit, brisket, pulled pork, braised chicken—you get the idea.

If you want to make them ahead of time, the uncooked lamb quenelles can be stored in the freezer for up to two months. On the day of service, simply take them out and immediately move to the next step. Have everything ready to go before those guys come out of the icebox.

In a food processor, pulse the still-warm meat and parsley for 30 seconds, then add the pistachios and process for an additional 30 seconds. With the processor running, slowly drizzle the warm fat into the processor. Continue processing until the mixture becomes dough-like—it should form into a ball that rotates around the processor. Add the egg and process for 15 to 30 seconds. Taste and season lightly with salt—remembering that the fat and the braised meat are already seasoned. (I suggest you start with ¼ teaspoon and add more if needed.)

Quenelles can be formed two ways: the traditional, classic way, using two spoons, or the easy way, using an ice cream scoop. The ice cream scoop method works

well, though the quenelles will not be as pretty as those formed using the classic method.

To form quenelles the easy way: Roll the edge of an ice cream scoop along the top of your mixture. Gently fill the scoop about halfway, forming a basic quenelle that can be now be put on a sheet tray to freeze.

To form them the classic way: Get two same-sized spoons and a cup of warm water. The size of the spoon determines the size of the quenelles; for this recipe, use a dinner spoon. With one spoon, scoop up a generous spoonful of the mixture (it's easier to form quenelles when there's more mixture in the spoon). Using the inside, concave surface of the other spoon, push the mixture back onto the opposite spoon while turning your hand around the lamb mixture, holding onto the angle and creating a sharp edge to the quenelle. Dip the first spoon into the warm water and push the mixture back into that spoon while rotating. Repeat a few times until the quenelle is formed. (It will look like a little football.)

This isn't the easiest thing to get down. I was mocked incessantly for my horrible quenelles at the restaurant where I worked under a sous chef (Eric Brown, a certified badass and now a great friend) who could quenelle a Muscat grape puree with his eyes closed

better than I could with my eyes open—which he did just to prove how awful I was. But with practice you'll figure it out, and it's a skill you will have forever.

Chill the formed quenelles in the freezer for 25 minutes. Keep them separated on a sheet pan so they don't stick together. Don't skip this step; chilling the quenelles lets the egg wash and almond flour stick and keeps the lamb from overcooking when you fry it.

Once the quenelles have chilled, begin heating the oil. Fill a pan (I like to use a 12-inch cast iron pan) so the oil reaches ½ inch up the sides, and set it over medium heat.

In a medium bowl, whisk together the egg and the water. Place the flour in another bowl.

One by one, roll the quenelles in the egg mixture and then gently roll in the almond flour.

When the surface of the oil looks wavy and a couple pinches of almond flour fry up quickly, the oil is ready. (If you're checking with a thermometer, 325°F is the perfect temp.) Fry the quenelles for about 2 minutes per side, or until golden-brown. Transfer the finished ones to a plate lined with paper towels and hit them with a pinch of salt.

LAMB MEATBALLS

SERVES 4 · YIELD 10 TO 12 MEATBALLS · COOK TIME 25 MINUTES

INGREDIENTS

2 POUNDS GROUND LAMB

1 SMALL YELLOW ONION, CUT INTO SMALL DICE (¾ CUP)

3 TABLESPOONS OLIVE OIL

2 TABLESPOONS BALSAMIC VINEGAR

1 TABLESPOON FINELY CHOPPED FRESH THYME

1 TABLESPOON FINELY CHOPPED FRESH OREGANO

½ TABLESPOON FRESHLY GROUND BLACK PEPPER

1 TABLESPOON SALT

1 RECIPE ROASTED SPAGHETTI SQUASH (PAGE 176), FOR SERVING (OPTIONAL)

1 RECIPE ARTICHOKE AND TOMATO SAUCE, SPREAD, DIP (PAGE 224), FOR SERVING (OPTIONAL)

Preheat the oven to 375°F.

Combine all the ingredients in a bowl and mix well by hand. Form into 2-ounce meatballs; they should be a little larger than a golf ball.

Place in a 9-by-13-inch baking dish, uncovered. Bake for 20 to 25 minutes, or until golden-brown and firm to the touch. The internal temperature should be 155°F.

These are great over spaghetti squash, especially topped with Artichoke and Tomato Sauce, Spread, Dip (page 224), as shown.

There's an easy way to test the doneness of meat by touch. Touch your pointer finger to the thumb on the same hand and with your other hand feel the fleshy part under your thumb. Now touch your middle finger to your thumb and feel that muscle stiffen. That's what rare to medium rare meat should feel like. Use your ring finger for medium, the pinky for medium well, and for well-done . . . touch your shoe.

BISON BOLOGNESE

SERVES 4 · COOK TIME 1 HOUR

INGREDIENTS

½ POUND PANCETTA

1 SMALL YELLOW ONION, DICED

½ POUND CHICKEN LIVER, PUREED

1 POUND GROUND BISON

2 TABLESPOONS CHOPPED GARLIC

1 TABLESPOON SALT, PLUS MORE TO TASTE

1 (28-OUNCE) CAN CRUSHED SAN MARZANO TOMATOES

½ TABLESPOON CHOPPED FRESH OREGANO

½ TABLESPOON CHOPPED FRESH THYME

SALT

1 RECIPE ROASTED SPAGHETTI SQUASH (PAGE 176), FOR SERVING

● ●

Roughly chop the pancetta into 1-inch pieces and lightly pulse in a food processor until shredded to the size of rice. Heat a large cast iron frying pan over medium heat; add the pancetta to the dry, hot pan to brown and render the fat.

When the pancetta begins to turn light golden-brown, after about 8 minutes, add the diced onion and sauté for another 8 minutes. Add pureed chicken liver, stir well, and cook for 2 minutes. Add the bison, stir well, and add the garlic and salt; sauté for 8 minutes. Add the tomatoes, reduce heat to medium-low, and simmer for 30 minutes, stirring every 10 minutes or so.

Finish with the fresh oregano and thyme and add salt to taste. Serve over spaghetti squash.

CORNISH GAME HEN AND ROULADES

SERVES 4 · COOK TIME 1 HOUR

This recipe is perfect for when you want to spend some time in the kitchen making something very special. The leftover game hen mixture can be used for meatballs or meat loaf.

The game hen and roulades are excellent served with New Potatoes with Kale (page 230) or Celery Root Salad (page 238).

INGREDIENTS

2 CORNISH GAME HENS

2 TABLESPOONS OLIVE OIL

1 LEEK, WHITE PART ONLY, ROUGHLY CHOPPED

1 TEASPOON FRESH THYME

¼ CUP ROUGHLY CHOPPED CARROTS

1 EGG

1 TEASPOON SALT

1 TEASPOON FRESHLY GROUND BLACK PEPPER

The bones and scraps make a delicious stock. Roast the bones at 400°F until golden-brown, add them to a stockpot with the carrot peelings and the leek scraps, fill the pot with water, and make stock while you are preparing the rest of the dish.

Butcher the Cornish game hens (see instructions on page 21) and debone the thighs and legs. Keep the skin on the breasts and set them aside for later. Carefully remove the skin from the thighs and the legs and cut it into 3- or 4-inch squares; you will use them to roll the roulades.

In a food processor, combine all the ingredients, including the meat, and process to a slightly chunky texture—it should take about five pulses. While the mixture shouldn't be perfectly smooth, you also don't want large chunks or you won't be able to roll it well. Aim for the texture of sausage filling.

Drop a tablespoon of the meat mixture into a hot sauté pan or skillet over medium-high heat to test the seasoning. Cook through, taste, and adjust the flavor as needed before rolling the roulades.

Lay out two pieces of plastic wrap about 12 inches long by 14 inches wide. You'll need two sheets, but lay them out one at a time and place a piece of skin in the center of each piece. Stretch out the skin so it is nice and flat.

Place just over a tablespoon of the filling near the edge of the skin that is closest to you and form it into a line. Don't spread the filling all the way to the edges of the skin.

Carefully roll up the skin, making sure the filling doesn't squeeze out the edges. Wrap it in the plastic wrap, twist the ends of the wrap to tighten, and use the holding power of the plastic wrap to form it into firm roulades. Place two plastic-wrapped sausages in each vacuum-sealed bag or small Ziploc bag with all the air removed.

Set the immersion circulator at 145°F to 150°F. If you don't have an immersion circulator, bring a medium pot of water to just under 150°F. You want it warm enough to cook the meat but not so hot that it renders the fat from the skin.

Cook the roulades for 30 minutes, remove them from the immersion circulator or pot of water, and place them in an ice bath to chill. Let them firm up, still wrapped, in the fridge for at least an hour. When you're ready to cook them, carefully remove the roulades from the plastic wrap.

To cook the breast and the roulades, heat a dry cast iron pan over medium-high heat. I suggest cooking two breasts and two roulades at one time. On each roulade, find where the skin comes together and cook that side first, then sear all the way around.

Once the roulades start to brown, add the breast, skin side down. Hold it down with your fingers, because the skin will try to buckle on you. Cook on the skin side for 4 to 5 minutes, until it's nice and crispy, then flip and cook on the other side for an additional 3 to 4 minutes. The roulades and the breast should be done at the same time.

BRAISED SHORT RIBS WITH FENNEL AND SOUS VIDE CARROTS

SERVES 4 · COOK TIME 6½ HOURS

INGREDIENTS

5 TABLESPOONS OLIVE OIL, DIVIDED

1½ TEASPOON SALT, DIVIDED

1½ POUNDS SHORT RIBS, BONE IN

FRONDS AND STALKS FROM 1 BULB FENNEL, CHOPPED

1 LARGE YELLOW ONION, JULIENNED

2 CUPS REDUCED CHICKEN STOCK (PAGE 270; FOLLOW METHOD ON PAGE 213 FOR REDUCING)

½ TEASPOON FRESHLY GROUND BLACK PEPPER

½ CUP MINCED RAW FENNEL

1 TABLESPOON CHOPPED FRESH DILL

FOR THE CARROTS

2 QUARTS BEEF STOCK (PAGE 274)

1 BUNCH BABY CARROTS, PEELED (RESERVE THE PEELS FOR STOCK)

PINCH OF SALT

PINCH OF LEMON ZEST (ROUGHLY ⅛ TEASPOON)

1 TEASPOON OLIVE OIL

2 SMALL SPRIGS DILL

1 TABLESPOON FAT RESERVED FROM SHORT RIBS, OR GHEE

Each part of this meal has a lot of steps and processes. To make it a bit easier, try making regular roasted carrots the first time and then, once you're comfortable with the basic process for making the short ribs, try the sous vide method for the carrots. It helps to slowly build your repertoire before tackling everything at once.

This meal uses a few ingredients in many ways, layering and building the flavors. It is a good example of using and reusing every element to develop the dish. The carrots are cooked in stock made from the rib bones and fat from the braising liquid. The meal uses every element, wrapping and layering the flavors so that it has depth and complexity, despite its simplicity.

In my opinion, really great food is about layering and overlapping flavors as much as you can. Every time you find a way to use scraps or peelings instead of throwing them in the compost pile, you increase the flavor.

COOK THE RIBS

Preheat the oven to 300°F.

In a thick-bottomed Dutch oven or soup pot, heat 3 tablespoons of the olive oil over high heat until it's just short of smoking; you'll see it shimmer. Sprinkle with ½ teaspoon of the salt and add the short ribs. Cook until they're good and crusty brown on one side, about

6 minutes, and then flip them over and add the fennel fronds and onion. Let it sear for another 2 minutes.

Add the chicken stock; this will pull the short ribs off of the bottom of the pot. (If 2 cups of stock isn't enough to cover at least half the meat, add water until half the meat is covered in liquid.) Give it a good stir while scraping the bottom with a wooden spoon and add the remaining

1 teaspoon of salt and the black pepper. Bring to a simmer, cover, and cook in the oven for 5 hours.

Remove from the oven and allow to cool for 30 to 60 minutes. Skim the fat from the top and reserve for the carrots. Discard the pieces of fennel stems and fronds from the braising pan.

MAKE THE PATTIES

Pull the meat from the bones, reserving the bones for stock (see recipe on page 274). Mince the meat and mix in the fresh fennel and dill.

Lightly form the short rib mixture into patties. In a cast iron pan over high heat, add the remaining 2 tablespoons of olive oil and brown the patties for about 3 minutes on each side. When you flip the patties, make sure to use a spatula that is as wide as the patty, otherwise it will crumble.

REDUCE THE BEEF STOCK

Pour the beef stock into a medium saucepot and place the pot halfway over a burner set to medium-high heat. This creates convection—a current is formed in the stock when the heated parts begin to move—and the stock will begin to clarify. It's a pretty amazing process, similar to making a consommé.

As the stock begins to come to a low boil, a film will form on the top. Using a ladle, gently skim off the film and discard. A film will form again while it's reducing; remove each time.

Reduce to roughly ½ cup, about one-eighth of the original volume; this should take about 3 hours. Set aside 2 tablespoons for this recipe and freeze the rest. It will keep for up to 3 months.

SOUS VIDE THE CARROTS

Cut off the tops of the carrots, keeping about ½ inch of green at the top for color. Place the carrots, salt, lemon zest, olive oil, and dill in a sous vide bag or sealable plastic bag, expelling as much air as possible from the bag.

If you have sous vide equipment, you can use it to easily make the carrots: cook at 190°F for 1 hour. Most home cooks don't, however, so following are instructions for a makeshift stovetop sous vide station.

If you don't have sous vide equipment, let the carrots sit in the bag overnight before cooking; they will not absorb the flavors as fast when they are not under the vacuum seal of a sous vide bag. The next day, fill a medium or large stockpot about halfway with water and heat it over medium-low heat until the water is 195°F. At that temperature the water will steam and tiny bubbles will appear at the bottom, but it should only have a gentle simmer. There should not be a lot of motion to the water.

Once the water is at the desired temperature, submerge the bagged carrots in the water and let them cook slowly for 50 minutes.

GLAZE THE CARROTS

Heat a thick-bottomed sauté pan over medium-high heat and add the fat skimmed from the braising liquid for the short ribs. Remove the carrots from the bag and transfer them to the sauté pan. Cook the carrots for 2 minutes, carefully add the reduced beef stock, and shake the pan to move the carrots around. The carrots should glaze perfectly.

Serve the rib meat patties with the carrots, and enjoy!

STRIP STEAK

SERVES 4 · COOK TIME 8 TO 25 MINUTES

INGREDIENTS

4 (8-OUNCE) STRIP STEAKS

4 TABLESPOONS SALT

Lightly coat the steaks with the salt and allow to sit for 10 minutes.

If you are cooking on a gas grill, make sure the grill gets very hot. If you are using charcoal, wait until you have red-hot coals.

Place the four steaks parallel to each other with the tips at 2 o'clock. Cook for 2 minutes. Rotate 90 degrees counterclockwise, so the tips are at 10 o'clock, and cook for 2 minutes. This creates the classic hash marks.

Flip the steaks over and, starting with the tips at 10 o'clock, repeat the same steps to create the hash marks and delicious char flavor.

The steaks are "Pittsburgh rare" now, black and brown on the outside and purple-cool inside. If this is the desired level of doneness, remove from heat. Otherwise, move the steaks away from the direct heat on the grill and cover.

Cook according to the times at right.

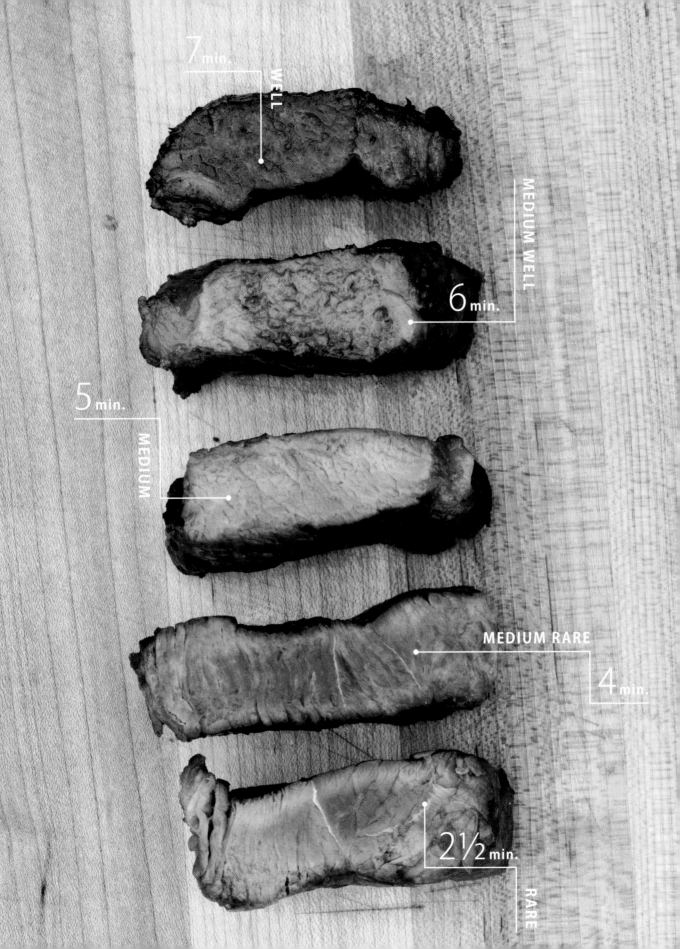

7 min. WELL

6 min. MEDIUM WELL

5 min. MEDIUM

MEDIUM RARE 4 min.

2½ min. RARE

CELERIAC PUREE

SERVES 4 · COOK TIME 40 MINUTES

INGREDIENTS

1 LARGE CELERIAC (2 POUNDS)

2¼ CUPS VEGETABLE STOCK, DIVIDED (SEE NOTES)

1 TEASPOON SALT

1 TABLESPOON COLD BACON FAT (SEE NOTES)

* Notes: The color of the stock will affect the color of the puree. So using a stock without carrots or other dark vegetables will give you a lighter-colored puree.

For this recipe, you can use clarified butter or bacon fat; just make sure it is cold and solid when you add it.

While it's delicious on its own, this dish also makes the base for an amazing soup: just add extra stock and top it with crispy bacon lardons, celery leaves fried in bacon fat for just a few seconds, and a coarse ground of black pepper.

Celeriac isn't used as often as it should be. Hand-mashed with a bit of vegetable stock, some ghee or bacon fat, and ¼ cup of diced chives, it's is so good that you won't want potatoes for a month afterward. Or peel it, chop it into medium dice, and combine it with equal parts butternut squash, rutabaga, and turnips and four or five large halved shallots. Coat with olive oil, season with salt and pepper, and roast at 375°F for 25 to 30 minutes, until golden-brown and delicious. Toss with fresh thyme or oregano. It's a simple, delicious way to enjoy winter vegetables.

A high-speed blender is best for this recipe; a food processor won't get you the silky texture that defines this dish. That said, you can get the job done with an immersion blender in a high-sided mixing container or with a regular blender. It'll work; the texture just won't be quite as smooth.

Cut off the top and bottom of the celeriac. Working on a flat surface, peel the celeriac with a santuko or utility knife (a short, 4- to 5-inch blade with no serration or bevel) and then cut it into large dice.

Place the celeriac, 2 cups of the stock, and the salt in a medium saucepan, cover, and bring to a boil over high heat. Reduce the heat but continue to boil, covered, for 30 minutes, then remove the lid and boil for an additional 5 minutes. The celeriac should be soft and the liquid reduced by at least half; if not, continue boiling uncovered.

Make sure the bacon fat is cold when you add it. This is the key to emulsifying the vegetable mixture. It's the same technique used to make a classic butter, or mounted, sauce. You remove the pan from the heat just before slowly adding the cold butter, bit by bit, while steadily stirring the pan. The butter emulsifies into the sauce, creating a silky sauce that shines. It looks beautiful and tastes amazing. A fat emulsion like this is all that's right with the world. If the sauce is too hot or the butter isn't cold enough, it will break. Take the time to do it right.

Place the celeriac mixture and remaining ¼ cup of stock in a high-speed blender and begin to process. With the blender on, add the cold fat in small pieces—this gives you the best emulsification. Blend until silky smooth.

ROASTED BEETS WITH SALSIFY AND FENNEL FRONDS

SERVES 6 · COOK TIME 2 HOURS TO ROAST THE BEETS, 30 MINUTES TO POACH THE SALSIFY

This is one of those simple salads that you can make using leftover roasted root vegetables. You can warm all the ingredients through gently in a pan or toss all of it cold in a bowl. Either way, it's quite good and a perfect winter dish.

INGREDIENTS

2 HERB-ROASTED BEETS (ABOUT 1 POUND; PAGE 234), PEELED AND CUT INTO ½-INCH DICE

½ RECIPE OIL-POACHED SALSIFY (PAGE 222), CUT INTO 1-INCH PIECES

2 TABLESPOONS CHOPPED FRESH FENNEL FRONDS OR DILL

1 TABLESPOON APPLE CIDER VINEGAR

1 TABLESPOON OLIVE OIL

2 TEASPOONS SALT

¼ TEASPOON FRESHLY GROUND BLACK PEPPER

● ● ●

In a serving bowl, toss together all of the ingredients. Serve as a base for Lamb Quenelles (page 202), as shown, or as a side.

OIL-POACHED SALSIFY

SERVES 6 • COOK TIME 30 MINUTES

Salsify is to Belgium what celeriac is to Britain: the unofficial national root vegetable. Salsify is delicate, sweet, and slightly piney on its own, but it is also a great vessel for other flavors and textures, as in this recipe.

Poaching in olive oil is a great medium for flavor development and infusion, and combining it with salsify gives this recipe many possible variations. You could add different herbs, such as thyme or sage, or add some chili flakes and star anise to give it a real Vietnamese flavor. Have fun trying other seasonings; in the process you'll have learned another cooking method in another cooking medium.

This dish can be served hot or cold. I like to toss salsify in a medley of root vegetables, and it's a really great addition to soups. This is what winter is about: cooking with a bunch of vegetables that you've never heard of and that it takes a sharp knife to get through.

Peel the salsify with a vegetable peeler and cut into 1-inch pieces.

In a 12-inch cast iron frying pan, heat the oil and add the salsify, rosemary, garlic, lemon, salt, and black pepper. The ingredients will float towards the top of the oil; give it a good stir every couple minutes while it's cooking. The ideal oil temperature is 285°F, at which point there will be a good consistent bubble coming off the pan contents and oil without it looking like a fryer. Continue to poach with the oil barely simmering for 30 minutes.

*Note: When purchasing salsify, look for a firm, thick root. Make sure it feels as if it would break, not bend, if pressed. Store unpeeled in your produce bin and use within two weeks.

INGREDIENTS

2 POUNDS SALSIFY (SEE NOTE)

2 CUPS OLIVE OIL

2 SPRIGS FRESH ROSEMARY

2 CLOVES GARLIC, PEELED

1 LEMON, SLICED

1 TEASPOON SALT

1 TEASPOON FRESHLY GROUND BLACK PEPPER

When poaching with oil, as in this recipe, you need to have a much lower temperature than when frying. Frying generally happens at over 300°F, while poaching should be done at around 285°F—a big difference that has a huge impact.

ARTICHOKE AND TOMATO SAUCE, SPREAD, DIP

YIELD 3 CUPS

This is a versatile dipping sauce: it's perfect for crudité platters, on top of fish or chicken, or for folding into sautéed vegetables. This recipe makes a big batch that you can use throughout the week.

Tomatoes are summer vegetables, but since this recipe is made with canned tomatoes and artichokes, you can make it any time of year. With a greenhouse or window box, you can even have fresh basil year-round.

Process the artichoke hearts and tomatoes in two batches in a food processor, starting with half of the tomatoes, half of the artichokes, 1 clove garlic, and 1/4 cup basil. Pulse into a finely chopped texture and repeat.

Mix the two batches in a large bowl and taste before adding salt. Each brand of canned tomatoes and artichokes has a different amount of added salt, so you may not need to add any more. Place in glass jars and store in the refrigerator. Use within 1 week.

INGREDIENTS

1 (12-OUNCE) CAN QUARTERED ARTICHOKE HEARTS, WELL DRAINED

1 (12-OUNCE) CAN WHOLE PEELED TOMATOES, WELL DRAINED

2 CLOVES GARLIC

½ CUP FRESH BASIL LEAVES

SALT

SPICY ASIAN SLAW

SERVES 4 · COOK TIME 30 MINUTES TO CHILL

INGREDIENTS

1 HEAD NAPA CABBAGE, SLICED

1 JALAPEÑO PEPPER, SEEDED AND CHOPPED (KEEP THE SEEDS IN FOR MORE SPICE)

¼ CUP SLICED SCALLIONS

¼ CUP CHOPPED CILANTRO

1 TABLESPOON FISH SAUCE (SEE NOTE)

1 TABLESPOON CIDER VINEGAR

1 TABLESPOON TOASTED SESAME OIL

½ TABLESPOON SALT

½ TABLESPOON FRESHLY GROUND BLACK PEPPER

●

In a large bowl, mix together all the ingredients.

Refrigerate for 30 minutes before serving.

* Note: Red Boat brand is the best Paleo fish sauce out there.

CAST IRON WILTED KALE

SERVES 4 · COOK TIME 10 MINUTES

INGREDIENTS

2 TABLESPOONS GHEE

1 SMALL YELLOW ONION, JULIENNED

PINCH OF SALT, PLUS MORE TO TASTE

1 BUNCH KALE, JULIENNED

FRIED CELERY LEAF, FOR GARNISH

Heat the ghee in a large cast iron pan over medium-high heat. Let it heat for a couple minutes; you want it nice and hot.

Add the onion and salt and let cook, without stirring, for at least a couple minutes. Once you see a nice char develop, stir it once and continue cooking for about 4 minutes, or until it starts to develop a crust, then add the kale. Let it cook for 2 minutes, then stir.

Remove from heat and stir well for about 1 minute. Season with salt to taste. For garnish, fry a celery leaf: drop it into oil heated to 300°F for five seconds and then let it rest on a paper towel to drain.

GLAZED SWEET POTATOES

SERVES 4 • COOK TIME 30 MINUTES

INGREDIENTS

3 MEDIUM SWEET POTATOES (ABOUT 8 OUNCES EACH), CUT INTO STRIPS

4 TABLESPOONS OLIVE OIL, DIVIDED

½ CUP CHICKEN STOCK (PAGE 270), ROOM TEMPERATURE

SALT

Preheat the oven to 400°F.

Coat the sweet potatoes with 2 tablespoons of the olive oil and place them on a sheet pan. Bake for 20 minutes.

Just before serving, brown and glaze the sweet potatoes: Heat the remaining 2 tablespoons of olive oil in a thick-bottomed sauté pan over medium-high heat. Once the oil is hot, add the sweet potatoes.

After 5 minutes, the potatoes should begin to turn a deep golden-brown. Give them a good stir and allow them to brown a few minutes more. Once they are golden-brown and cooked through, add the stock. The sweet potatoes should glaze up perfectly. Use more stock if needed; the potatoes tend to soak up more stock than you'd think. Just make sure it's at room temperature when you use it. Add salt to taste.

NEW POTATOES WITH KALE

SERVES 4 · COOK TIME 35 MINUTES

INGREDIENTS

1 POUND NEW POTATOES

2 TABLESPOONS OLIVE OIL

½ CUP CHICKEN STOCK (PAGE 270)

2 CUPS THINLY SLICED KALE

¼ TEASPOON SALT

¼ TEASPOON FRESHLY GROUND BLACK PEPPER

In a stockpot, boil the potatoes till they are fork-tender, 15 to 20 minutes. Remove from heat, rinse with cold water, and slice in half.

Heat the olive oil in a thick-bottomed sauté pan over medium heat. Once the oil is hot, add the potatoes. It can be a little tedious, but put all the potatoes in the pan with the cut side down.

Once the potatoes are going, add the chicken stock to a small saucepot over medium-high heat, bring it to just under a boil at around 185°F, and let simmer while the potatoes finish.

After about 10 minutes, the potatoes develop a deep golden-brown color on the flat side (you'll see the edges start to brown). Give them a quick stir, add the kale, stir well, cook for 1 minute, and then add the hot stock. The potatoes should glaze up perfectly. Season with the salt and pepper.

BRAISED CIPOLLINI

SERVES 4 · COOK TIME 40 MINUTES

INGREDIENTS

· 8 TO 12 CIPOLLINI ONIONS

½ TEASPOON SALT

½ TEASPOON FRESHLY GROUND BLACK PEPPER

1 CUP CHICKEN STOCK (PAGE 270)

Preheat the oven to 350°F.

Remove the tops and bottoms of the cipollini, leaving just a bit of the stem and root to hold it together. Make a slit into the outermost layer and remove it.

Place the cipollini, salt, and pepper in an oven-safe pan and cover halfway with the chicken stock. Place the pan on the stovetop and bring to a simmer, then cover and braise in the oven for 35 to 40 minutes.

HERB-ROASTED BEETS

SERVES 10 · COOK TIME 2 HOURS

This recipe lets you roast a lot of beets at once, which you can then use as a base for any number of recipes or ideas—such as Romaine, Radish, and Roasted Beet Salad (page 134); Roasted Beets with Salsify and Fennel Fronds (page 220); Beet Gratin (page 236); or Beet Puree (page 236).

Beets are so delicious and versatile, but they are not a spur-of-the-moment vegetable. It's worthwhile to make a batch this size and use it throughout the week in various dishes. Roasted beets will last a week in the fridge.

INGREDIENTS

4 TO 5 MEDIUM BEETS (7 TO 8 OUNCES EACH)

1 YELLOW ONION, ROUGHLY CHOPPED

4 SPRIGS FRESH THYME, DIVIDED

¾ TEASPOON SALT, DIVIDED

¾ TEASPOON FRESHLY GROUND BLACK PEPPER, DIVIDED

Preheat the oven to 350°F.

Place the whole beets, onion, 3 sprigs of the thyme, ½ teaspoon of the salt, and ½ teaspoon of the pepper in a shallow 9-by-13-inch baking dish and add 2 to 3 inches of water. Cover with a lid or plastic wrap and foil.

Roast for 2 hours, or until the beets are tender—a knife stuck in them should easily slip out. Place the beets in an ice bath for 10 minutes, then use a paper towel to slip the skins off of the beets. They should come off easily.

Chop the remaining sprig of thyme and cut the beets into ½-inch dice. Toss together the beets, chopped thyme, and the remaining ¼ teaspoon of salt and ¼ teaspoon of pepper.

BEET PUREE

SERVES 4 · COOK TIME 10 MINUTES, PLUS 2 HOURS TO ROAST THE BEET

INGREDIENTS

1 MEDIUM HERB-ROASTED BEET (PAGE 234), ROUGHLY CHOPPED

SALT

Place the beet in a shallow baking dish and add just enough water to cover it. Cook over high heat at a rolling boil until the water has almost completely evaporated, about 10 minutes.

Transfer the beet and liquid from the pan to a high-speed blender and puree. Alternatively, place it in a bowl and use an immersion blender to puree. You can also, if you want it to be as silky as possible, push the puree through a fine mesh strainer: using a rubber spatula and holding the strainer over a bowl, spoon the puree into the strainer and push it through. Season with salt to taste.

BEET GRATIN

SERVES 4 · COOK TIME 8 MINUTES, PLUS 2 HOURS TO ROAST THE BEETS

INGREDIENTS

1 TO 2 TABLESPOONS GHEE

1 SMALL YELLOW ONION, FINELY DICED OR BRUNOISED

4 CUPS BEET GREENS, STEMMED AND CHIFFONADED

PINCH OF SALT

2 TO 3 HERB-ROASTED BEETS (PAGE 234), THINLY SLICED

FRESH DILL, FOR GARNISH

OLIVE OIL, FOR GARNISH

In a large cast iron pan, heat the ghee over medium-high heat. Once the ghee is almost smoking, after about 3 to 4 minutes, add the onion and sauté without stirring until translucent, about 2 minutes. Add the beet greens and cook without stirring for a minute or two, add the salt, and remove from heat. Stir well and use the retained heat in the pan to continue cooking the beet greens until they cool.

On a serving plate, stack alternating layers of the beets and the beet greens. Stack the beets and greens four or five levels high and garnish with fresh dill and a drizzle of olive oil. Make sure you stack the largest slices with on the bottom and the smallest on the top. Varying the sizes makes for more of a pile of beets and greens than a plated gratin.

CELERY ROOT SALAD

SERVES 4 • COOK TIME 2 TO 4 HOURS TO MARINATE

INGREDIENTS

2 CUPS PEELED AND JULIENNED CELERY ROOT

1 CUP THINLY SLICED KUMQUATS

2 TABLESPOONS OLIVE OIL

½ TABLESPOON BALSAMIC VINEGAR

JUICE OF 1 SMALL NAVEL ORANGE

½ TABLESPOON FRESH MARJORAM LEAVES

1 TEASPOON SALT

½ TEASPOON FRESHLY GROUND BLACK PEPPER

In a large bowl, mix together all the ingredients. Add another pinch of salt to continue to pull moisture while it's in the fridge. Place in the fridge and allow to marinate for 2 to 4 hours. Serve chilled.

SWEET POTATO AND APPLE SALAD

SERVES 4 · COOK TIME 5 MINUTES, PLUS OVERNIGHT TO MARINATE

INGREDIENTS

1 GALA, FUJI, OR PINK LADY APPLE, FINELY DICED OR BRUNOISED

2 TABLESPOONS APPLE CIDER VINEGAR

1 TABLESPOON LEMON JUICE

1 TABLESPOON GHEE

1 POUND PURPLE SWEET POTATOES, FINELY DICED OR BRUNOISED

Marinate the apples in the apple cider vinegar and lemon juice overnight in the refrigerator. This creates a very cool effect where the apples are translucent and look cooked but are still crunchy and raw. If you're a super food nerd and have a vacuum sealer, you can get the same effect in 5 minutes by putting the apples under pressure.

The next day, heat the ghee in a thick-bottomed sauté pan over medium-high heat. Once the ghee is almost smoking, add the potatoes and pan fry, stirring every 30 seconds or so, until they turn a light golden-brown, about 3 minutes.

Remove the potatoes from the heat and transfer them to a bowl. Add the cold apples and mix to arrest the cooking process. For a super fancy presentation, form the potato and apple mixture into quenelles using the method on page 204 (if you don't have this down, portioning the mixture with a spoon is fine as well), but it's beautiful and delicious spooned into a bowl, too.

CANDIED BACON AND APPLE SALAD

SERVES 4 • COOK TIME 8 MINUTES

Candied bacon is the perfect sweet-salty touch for this winter salad, but it's also great for dessert, chilled and dipped in melted semisweet chocolate. It's a finicky dish that requires precision, though, so pay close attention to the oven settings and cook times.

INGREDIENTS

8 OUNCES BACON

½ CUP COCONUT SUGAR

½ GALA, PINK LADY, OR FUJI APPLE (4 OUNCES), THINLY SLICED

1 TABLESPOON OLIVE OIL

SQUEEZE OF LEMON

1 TO 2 TEASPOONS CHOPPED PARSLEY

● ● ● ●

If you're workng with full slab bacon, freeze it so you can slice it super thin.

Preheat the oven to 367°F.

First, make the candied bacon: Slice the bacon into thin strips, place it on a silpat or a wax paper–lined sheet pan, and generously cover with the coconut sugar. Place another silpat or a second layer of wax paper on top and then a sheet pan on top of that, to keep everything flat while cooking. Cook in the oven for 8 minutes. Remove from oven and let cool for 10 minutes. Slice into long triangles or "shards" by slicing diagonally along the bacon. Set aside 2 ounces of bacon for the salad and store the rest in the freezer for up to 3 months.

In a medium bowl toss together the apple slices, olive oil, lemon juice, parsley, and the 2 ounces of candied bacon.

BRAISED LAMB AND KALE SALAD

SERVES 6 • COOK TIME 15 MINUTES, PLUS 3 HOURS TO BRAISE THE LAMB

INGREDIENTS

1 CUP QUARTERED RADISHES (SEE NOTE)

1½ TABLESPOONS GHEE, DIVIDED

1 HEAD MAITAKE MUSHROOMS, BOTTOM CUT OFF AND BROKEN APART

PINCH OF SALT

¾ CUP QUARTERED ARTICHOKE HEARTS (6 OUNCES), COOKED

¼ CUP SHAVED SHALLOTS

1 HEAD DINOSAUR KALE, STEMMED AND CHIFFONADED

2 CUPS BRAISED LAMB (PAGE 198)

½ CUP MARCONA ALMONDS

2 TO 3 TABLESPOONS BONE MARROW VINAIGRETTE (PAGE 266)

● ●

While you prepare the rest of the salad, soak the radishes in cold water to keep them crisp and soften their spiciness.

Heat 1 tablespoon of the ghee in a cast iron pan over high heat. Once the ghee is hot, add the maitake mushrooms and a pinch of salt. Cook for 7 minutes, stirring occasionally. Add the artichoke hearts and the remaining ½ tablespoon of ghee, and cook for another 5 minutes, or until the artichoke hearts and maitake develop a deep golden color.

Add the shallots, stir, and after about 30 seconds add the kale. Don't let the shallots cook for long, since you don't want them to cook down and caramelize. Fold everything together in a minute or less and turn off the heat.

Add the lamb, radishes, Marcona almonds, and vinaigrette. Toss and serve with additional vinaigrette on the side in a warm cast iron pan. Make sure to serve the salad slightly warm or at room temperature. If you need to reheat the dish, freshen up the salad by adding a touch more dressing.

* Note: When prepping the radishes, don't cut them too small; you don't want to lose their color. And with this dish, you have the heavy kale and soft lamb, so the radishes provide a big, clean, cold crunch to balance them out.

These Paleo versions of the classics can be used throughout the year. Play with the flavors and adjust the recipes based on what is in season.

CONDIMENTS

KETCHUP

YIELD 5 TO 6 CUPS • COOK TIME 1½ HOURS

INGREDIENTS

3 TABLESPOONS OLIVE OIL

¾ POUND CARROTS, PEELED AND SLICED INTO ¼-INCH-THICK ROUNDS (3 CUPS)

½ CUP ROUGHLY CHOPPED YELLOW ONION

1 TABLESPOON PLUS 2½ TEASPOONS SALT, DIVIDED

1 TABLESPOON PEELED AND ROUGHLY CHOPPED GINGER

4 CLOVES GARLIC, ROUGHLY CHOPPED (2 TABLESPOONS)

2 TABLESPOONS SEEDED AND ROUGHLY CHOPPED RED JALAPEÑO PEPPER

1 TEASPOON GROUND CORIANDER

1½ TEASPOONS DRIED OREGANO

1½ POUNDS CHERRY TOMATOES, HALVED (SEE NOTES)

3 TABLESPOONS APPLE CIDER VINEGAR

3 POUNDS HEIRLOOM TOMATOES, ROUGHLY CHOPPED (SEE NOTES)

* Notes: You do not need to seed or chop the tops off of the tomatoes because the long cooking time and sieving will remove all the seeds and skin. Although you can use canned tomatoes, I suggest making this in the summer when tomatoes are in their peak season.

I suggest using purple cherry tomatoes if you can; they have fantastic flavor.

In a large saucepan, heat the oil over medium-high heat. Once the oil is hot, add the carrots, onion, and 1 tablespoon of the salt. Cook for 15 minutes, stirring occasionally, until lightly browned. (You want to pull the sugar from the vegetables, which requires some browning.)

Reduce the heat to medium and add the ginger, garlic, and jalapeño; simmer for 2 minutes. Add the coriander, oregano, and 1½ teaspoons of the salt and simmer for 2 minutes. Add the cherry tomatoes and simmer for 2 more minutes. Add the vinegar and continue to simmer for 12 minutes.

Add the heirloom tomatoes and the remaining teaspoon of salt and simmer for 25 minutes. Remove the pan from the heat and puree the mixture in the pan with an immersion blender. Alternatively, puree in batches using a food processor or blender. Strain through a sieve to remove seeds and any other particles.

Pour the strained mixture into a large saucepan and return to medium heat (if using the same saucepan, give it a quick rinse first). Bring to a simmer, reduce heat to low to maintain the simmer, and reduce the mixture for 20 to 30 minutes, or until you have a ketchup consistency. Keep the pan partially covered so you don't end up with tomato splatters all over the kitchen.

Allow the ketchup to cool to room temperature, then place in glass jars. It will keep in the refrigerator for 2 weeks.

MUSTARD

YIELD ABOUT 2 CUPS · COOK TIME 24 HOURS TO MARINATE

INGREDIENTS

1 CUP YELLOW MUSTARD SEEDS (5 OUNCES)

⅔ CUP APPLE CIDER VINEGAR

⅔ CUP WHITE WINE OR WATER

½ TEASPOON CORIANDER SEEDS

½ TEASPOON DRIED TARRAGON

1 TEASPOON SALT

½ TEASPOON GROUND TURMERIC

Place all the ingredients in a glass jar, seal, and allow to sit for 24 hours at room temperature.

Pour the entire mixture into a food processor or blender. Puree on high for 30 seconds for fine mustard or just pulse lightly for a more whole-grain texture.

Store in glass jars in the refrigerator for 2 to 3 weeks.

To keep the mustard, or anything else for that matter, fresh in your fridge for an extended period of time, don't contaminate it with any dirty spoons.

CHIMICHURRI SAUCE

YIELD 1 CUP

Use this on eggs, with meat, as a marinade, on fish. It's really awesome with almost anything.

Place all the ingredients in a blender, turn the blender on low, and then increase the speed to high. Continue to blend on high for 30 seconds. Store in a glass jar in the refrigerator for 3 to 5 days.

INGREDIENTS

3 CUPS PACKED CILANTRO

2 CUPS PACKED CURLY PARSLEY

½ SMALL RED ONION, ROUGHLY CHOPPED (½ CUP)

1½ TABLESPOONS ROUGHLY CHOPPED GARLIC

ZEST OF 1 LIME

JUICE OF 1 LIME

6 TABLESPOONS OLIVE OIL

2 TABLESPOONS RED WINE VINEGAR

½ TEASPOON FRESHLY GROUND BLACK PEPPER

½ TEASPOON SALT

ARUGULA PESTO

YIELD ABOUT 1¼ CUPS · COOK TIME 3 MINUTES

The lemon is very important in this recipe. Any green that is processed or broken down will oxidize and turn black, but the acid in the citrus keeps it green. If you do not have lemon, you can substitute a light-colored vinegar (I recommend champagne vinegar).

INGREDIENTS

4 TABLESPOONS PINE NUTS

4 CUPS PACKED ARUGULA

¾ TABLESPOON LEMON ZEST

1 TABLESPOON SLICED GARLIC

½ TEASPOON FRESHLY GROUND BLACK PEPPER

5 TABLESPOONS OLIVE OIL

2 TEASPOONS SALT

JUICE OF 1 LEMON

Dry roast the pine nuts: Heat a dry sauté pan over medium heat. Add the pine nuts and dry roast them pan for 2 to 3 minutes. Once they start to make a "snap, crackle, pop" noise, shake the pan back and forth or use a spatula to toss the nuts. Let the nuts sit for 30 seconds, then toss again; let sit for another 30 seconds, and toss again. Repeating the resting and tossing until the nuts are a light golden-brown color, 2 to 3 minutes total.

Remove the nuts from heat when you think they have 30 seconds to go, because they will continue to cook and darken in color. Immediately remove the pine nuts from the pan.

Add all the ingredients to a blender and process for approximately 30 seconds. If you go from low to high slowly, by the time you are at high, it should be just the right amount of time. This can also be done in a food processor.

Taste to make sure you are happy with the texture and blend longer if needed. The pesto will keep for 7 days in the fridge.

BACONNAISE

YIELD 1¼ TO 1½ CUPS

INGREDIENTS

½ CUP BACON FAT, IN LIQUID FORM AT ROOM TEMPERATURE

¾ CUP OLIVE OIL

2 LARGE EGG YOLKS

1 LARGE WHOLE EGG

¾ TEASPOON SALT

1 TEASPOON APPLE CIDER VINEGAR

Combine the bacon fat and oil in one measuring cup and set aside.

In a small metal bowl, use an immersion blender to blend (or whisk by hand) the egg yolks and whole egg until the mixture becomes milky white and frothy. When you see it change dramatically in color and texture, continue to mix a little longer. (This last bit of whisking is for added insurance, as it's at this stage that it's easy to stop blending too soon, and if the eggs aren't beaten enough, they cannot support the fat and emulsify into mayo.) Once the eggs are the desired consistency, begin to slowly add the oil mixture.

Continue to mix until all the oil is added, about 1 to 2 minutes. Season with the salt and vinegar, and add more to taste as desired.

While you can use a blender to make mayonnaise, I would only recommend that if you have a Vitamix or something of similar quality. Do not use a hand mixer— it will just make a huge mess.

ALMOND OIL MAYONNAISE

YIELD 1¼ CUPS

INGREDIENTS

2 LARGE EGG YOLKS

1 LARGE WHOLE EGG

1¼ CUPS ALMOND OIL

¾ TEASPOON SALT

1 TEASPOON APPLE CIDER VINEGAR

In a small metal bowl, use an immersion blender to blend (or whisk by hand) the egg yolks and whole egg until the mixture becomes milky white and frothy. When you see it change dramatically in color and texture, continue to mix a little longer. Once the eggs are the desired consistency, begin to slowly add the oil.

Continue to mix until all the oil is added. It should take approximately 1 to 2 minutes. Season with the salt and vinegar and add more to taste as desired.

ROASTED GARLIC MAYONNAISE

YIELD 1¼ CUPS • COOK TIME 20 MINUTES TO ROAST THE GARLIC

INGREDIENTS

2 LARGE EGG YOLKS

1 LARGE WHOLE EGG

1¼ CUPS OLIVE OIL

¾ TEASPOON SALT

1 TEASPOON APPLE CIDER VINEGAR

1 CLOVE RAW GARLIC, FINELY GRATED OR SENT THROUGH A GARLIC PRESS (AS A LAST RESORT)

1 CLOVE ROASTED GARLIC (SEE PAGE 58), SMASHED

In a small metal bowl, use an immersion blender to blend (or whisk by hand) the egg yolks and whole egg until the mixture becomes milky white and frothy. When you see it change dramatically in color and texture, continue to mix a little longer. Once the eggs are the desired consistency, begin to slowly add the oil. Continue to mix until all the oil is added. It should take approximately 1 to 2 minutes.

Season with the salt and vinegar. Add the raw and roasted garlic once the mayo has the proper consistency. Taste and add more seasoning if preferred.

TRUFFLE MAYONNAISE

YIELD 1¼ CUPS

INGREDIENTS

1 CUP OLIVE OIL

2 TABLESPOONS TRUFFLE OIL

2 LARGE EGG YOLKS

1 LARGE WHOLE EGG

¾ TEASPOON SALT

1 TEASPOON APPLE CIDER VINEGAR

Combine the olive oil and truffle oil in one measuring cup and set aside.

In a small metal bowl, use an immersion blender to blend (or whisk by hand) the egg yolks and whole egg until the mixture becomes milky white and frothy. When you see it change dramatically in color and texture, continue to mix a little longer. Once the eggs are the desired consistency, begin to slowly add the oil mixture. Continue to mix until all the oil is added. It should take approximately 1 to 2 minutes. Season with the salt and vinegar, and add more to taste as desired.

DUCK FAT MAYONNAISE

YIELD 1¼ CUPS

INGREDIENTS

½ CUP DUCK FAT, IN LIQUID FORM AT ROOM TEMPERATURE

¾ CUP OLIVE OIL

2 LARGE EGG YOLKS

1 LARGE WHOLE EGG

¾ TEASPOON SALT

1 TEASPOON APPLE CIDER VINEGAR

Combine the duck fat and oil in one measuring cup and set aside.

In a small metal bowl, use an immersion blender to blend (or whisk by hand) the egg yolks and whole egg until the mixture becomes milky white and frothy. When you see it change dramatically in color and texture, continue to mix a little longer. Once the eggs are the desired consistency, begin to slowly add the oil mixture. It should take approximately 1 to 2 minutes. Season with the salt and vinegar, then taste and add more as needed.

MARINARA SAUCE

SERVES 9 TO 10 · YIELD 4 QUARTS · COOK TIME 1 HOUR

INGREDIENTS

½ CUP ROUGHLY CHOPPED RAW PORK FAT

¾ POUND CARROTS, PEELED AND SLICED INTO ¼-INCH-THICK ROUNDS (3 CUPS)

1 SMALL YELLOW ONION (ABOUT 8 OUNCES), ROUGHLY CHOPPED

1 TABLESPOON PLUS 2 TEASPOONS SALT, DIVIDED

4 CLOVES GARLIC, ROUGHLY CHOPPED (2 TABLESPOONS)

2 TABLESPOONS SEEDED AND ROUGHLY CHOPPED RED JALAPEÑO PEPPER

1 TABLESPOON DRIED OREGANO

1½ POUNDS CHERRY TOMATOES, HALVED

1 TABLESPOON BALSAMIC VINEGAR

3 POUNDS HEIRLOOM TOMATOES, ROUGHLY CHOPPED (SEE NOTE)

1 CUP CHOPPED FRESH BASIL

* Note: For this recipe you will not be straining the mixture, so do make sure to cut the stem tops off the heirloom tomatoes. Although you can use canned tomatoes, I suggest making this in the summer when tomatoes are in their peak season.

Add the pork fat to a cold, large saucepan. Place the pan over medium heat and slowly render the fat, 6 to 7 minutes. Once the fat is rendered, increase the heat to medium-high and add the carrots, onion, and 1 tablespoon of the salt. Cook for 15 minutes over medium heat, stirring occasionally, until lightly browned. (You want to pull the sugar from the vegetables, so some light browning is needed.)

Reduce the heat to medium-low and add the garlic and jalapeño; cook for 2 minutes. Add the oregano and 1 teaspoon of the salt and cook for 2 minutes. Add the cherry tomatoes and simmer for 2 minutes. Add the vinegar and simmer for 12 minutes.

Add the heirloom tomatoes and the remaining 1 teaspoon of salt and simmer for 25 minutes, then fold in the basil. If you prefer a chunky sauce, you can use the sauce as-is. If you like a smooth texture, remove the pan from heat and puree in the pan with an immersion blender. Alternatiely, you can puree it in batches in a food processor or blender.

Carrot peels are a perfect example of useful scraps. Instead of throwing them away, you can make a quick and simple stock with them: in a stockpot, simmer the peelings from 5 carrots, a couple large chunks of yellow onion, 1 sprig fresh parsley, and 4 cups of cold water for 40 minutes, then strain.

BALSAMIC VINAIGRETTE

YIELD 1 CUP · COOK TIME 30 MINUTES TO REST

There are two rules you must never forget when making a vinaigrette: First, it needs to have a 3-to-1 fat-to-acid ratio. This is true for any fat—bacon fat, bone marrow, olive oil—and any acid—champagne vinegar, lime juice, whatever. The ratio never changes. Second, salt can't dissolve in fat, so mix it in with the vinegar when you start the dressing. With those two rules in mind, it's hard to go wrong.

In a small mixing bowl, combine the vinegar, salt, pepper, and mustard. Whisk together until the salt dissolves, then add the shallot and garlic. Slowly drizzle in the olive oil while whisking. Let stand for at least 30 minutes and whisk well before serving. The vinaigrette will keep for 30 days in the fridge.

INGREDIENTS

¼ CUP BALSAMIC VINEGAR

½ TEASPOON SALT

¼ TEASPOON FRESHLY GROUND BLACK PEPPER

½ TABLESPOON DIJON MUSTARD

½ SMALL SHALLOT, CHOPPED (1 TABLESPOON)

1 CLOVE GARLIC, MINCED (½ TABLESPOON)

¾ CUP EXTRA VIRGIN OLIVE OIL

BONE MARROW VINAIGRETTE

YIELD 1 CUP

Use a light-flavored olive oil with this recipe so the flavor of the bone marrow can shine through. You can find marrow bones at most butcher shops, and even some grocery stores have them towards the end of the meat aisle. But your best option is to use the marrow from bones that you've been braising (such as bones from the Braised Lamb on page 198).

In a food processor or blender, combine the vinegar, salt, pepper, and dill and pulse briefly. Add the bone marrow and blend for 30 seconds. While the blender is on, slowly drizzle in the olive oil. This will emulsify the mixture and create a full-bodied vinaigrette.

INGREDIENTS

2 TABLESPOONS APPLE CIDER VINEGAR

1 TEASPOON SALT

½ TEASPOON FRESHLY GROUND BLACK PEPPER

1 TABLESPOON FRESH DILL, MINT, OR CILANTRO (OR ANY LIGHT, CLEAN, FRESH HERB)

2 TABLESPOONS BONE MARROW

5 TABLESPOONS LIGHT OLIVE OIL

If you're not using bones from meat you've already cooked, roast them first at 450°F for 15 to 20 minutes. If the bones have been cut in half lengthwise, simply scoop out the marrow. If they've been cut crosswise, use the end of a chopstick to push out the marrow.

Although the terms are often used interchangeably, broths and stocks aren't the same thing. There is some debate on the exact definitions, but in general, stocks are made with bones, vegetables, and basic aromatics, such as carrots, onions, celery, thyme, bay leaf, and parsley. Broths, on the other hand, are made with more herbs—such as rosemary, cilantro, and mint—spices, salt, and meat.

Stocks are the secret weapon in every restaurant kitchen. Whenever you use water at home, restaurants use stock. This adds lots of gelatin, which has two benefits: it contains tons of great minerals and vitamins, and it adds mouth feel, making dishes silky and creating the sensation that food is bear-hugging your tongue. In every recipe that mentions using water for boiling, pureeing, or mashing, imagine how much deeper the flavor and richer the mouth feel would be if you used stock instead.

Always simmer stocks uncovered, and never add salt or garlic to a stock. Stocks are our base, our foundation. Once we are using them for a specific purpose or dish, we can begin seasoning and adding ingredients at will, but when making a foundation, it is best not to add any adjuncts like salt or garlic. Plus, very often you will be reducing stock and concentrating the flavor, so what tastes like the right amount of salt for one gallon of stock would be way too much once the stock is reduced by half.

When trying to decide how much stock to make, see what you have for storage containers. If you have 1½ gallons in containers, then that's how much you should make.

SIMMERING TIMES

Vegetables	40 minutes
Fish bones	1 hour
Shrimp shells	1 hour
Chicken bones	4 to 6 hours
Beef/veal/lamb bones	6 hours

Use 1 pound of vegetables for every gallon of liquid.

Use 1½ to 2 pounds of bones for every gallon of liquid.

STOCKS

HEARTY CHICKEN STOCK

YIELD 1 GALLON • COOK TIME 6 TO 8½ HOURS

I recommend you purchase a whole raw chicken, remove the meat from the carcass before cooking, and then use the bones to make stock. (See how to debone a chicken on page 21.)

You could ask the butcher to do this for you, but it's an important skill to have if you want to really know how to cook.

INGREDIENTS

3 POUNDS CHICKEN BACKS, BONES, AND FEET

1½ GALLONS COLD WATER

1 MEDIUM YELLOW ONION (12 TO 14 OUNCES), ROUGHLY CHOPPED

2 MEDIUM CARROTS (12 OUNCES), ROUGHLY CHOPPED

1 SPRIG FRESH PARSLEY

1 BAY LEAF

Preheat the oven to 400°F.

Roast the chicken bones on a sheet pan for 60 to 90 minutes, until they have a dark, roasted color. Remove from the oven and transfer the bones and all the drippings from the bottom of the pan to a large stockpot.

Add the cold water and bring to a simmer over medium heat. Move the pan so that it's only halfway on the burner. This creates a convection current that will help you skim the foam that collects on the top.

Allow to simmer, uncovered, for 1 hour without touching it and then skim all the foam from the top. Only skim once while cooking. Cook for a total of 4 to 6 hours, adding the onion, carrots, parsley, and bay leaf during the last hour of cooking.

Use a strainer to remove the bones, meat, and vegetables, and discard. Strain the remaining stock through a colander into a large storage container and let rest for an hour at room temperature. Store in the freezer for up to 3 months in freezer-safe Tupperware, or in the refrigerator for up to 10 days in a glass or plastic container.

SHRIMP STOCK OR BROTH

YIELD 1 QUART · COOK TIME 30 MINUTES OR 1 HOUR

INGREDIENTS

SHELLS FROM 1½ POUNDS SHRIMP

3 OUNCES BACON (OPTIONAL)

4 CUPS WATER

1 TEASPOON SALT

Combine all ingredients in a stockpot.

For stock, cook at a low simmer for 1 hour. This will make a translucent, more delicate, and softer liquid. For broth, cook at a rolling boil for 30 minutes. This will give it a deep flavor, and the results will be cloudy and slightly denser.

Strain and discard the solids.

BEEF STOCK

YIELD 1½ GALLONS · COOK TIME 5 HOURS

I don't use celery in my broths or stocks. I don't like it; it seems to give off a bitter flavor that just isn't right. But have at it if you feel the need.

INGREDIENTS

2 GALLONS COLD WATER

2 POUNDS BEEF FEMUR OR KNUCKLE BONES

2 LARGE ONIONS (1 POUND), ROUGHLY CHOPPED

2 CARROTS (8 OUNCES), ROUGHLY CHOPPED

1 BAY LEAF

1 BUNCH PARSLEY

Fill a big stockpot with the cold water and add the bones. Place the pot over medium heat. As the liquid warms, a film will appear on the surface. Skim it off with a ladle and discard. Do it this one more time while it comes up to a simmer. Simmer for 4 hours, but do not let it boil.

Add the onions, carrots, bay leaf, and parsley, and simmer for another hour. Strain and discard the solids. Let cool for an hour or two. Store in the freezer for up to 3 months.

If storage is an issue but you still want the added flavor of stock, you can reduce it to a demi-glace. After straining, continue simmering for about 4 more hours, until it is reduced to about 2 cups (15 percent of its original volume), always skimming the film as it comes to the top. Adding a tablespoon of this demi-glace to a pan of sautéed veggies or a soup will make it sing. Enjoy.

PHO BROTH

YIELD 1½ QUARTS · COOK TIME 30 MINUTES, PLUS 6 TO 8½ HOURS FOR CHICKEN STOCK

The key component of pho is the broth; the flavor from the Asian spices is what sets it apart. I use Chinese five-spice blend. It's an easy way to get the key flavors in one blend.

This broth can be made with almost any stock—pork, beef, veal, shrimp—but not fish, which just doesn't taste right.

If you're making pho in the wintertime and are using hefty winter vegetables such as winter squash, turnips, or rutabaga, I recommend using a roasted stock. For lighter spring and summer vegetables, such as bok choy, carrots, or zucchini, an unroasted stock is best.

If you do not have a gas burner on your stovetop, preheat a barbecue grill or cast iron stovetop grill to high, or set the oven rack in the top position and set the broiler to high.

Cut the onion in half and leave the ginger whole. Char them deeply on a grill, over the gas burner, or under the broiler, about 6 minutes.

Combine the charred vegetables, five-spice blend, and stock in a stockpot. Bring to a boil over medium-high heat and continue to boil for 20 minutes.

INGREDIENTS

1 SMALL YELLOW ONION (8 OUNCES), UNPEELED (REMOVE ONLY PAPERY OUTER SKIN)

1 (2-INCH) PIECE GINGER, UNPEELED

1 TABLESPOON CHINESE FIVE-SPICE POWDER

1½ QUARTS CHICKEN STOCK (PAGE 270)

Photo by Sean Coonce

BEEF CHART

7-Bone *Pot Roast*
Arm *Pot Roast*
Blade *Roast, Braise*
Under Blade *Pot Roast*
Chuck *Pot Roast*
Chuck Eye *Roast, Braise*
Short Ribs *Stew, Braise*
Flanken Style Ribs *Braise*
Mock Tender *Roast*
Chuck Top Blade Steak *Grill or Broil, Skillet*
Shoulder Top Blade Steak (Flat Iron) *Grill or Broil, Skillet*
Shoulder Petit Tender *Roast, Grill or Broil*
Shoulder Petite Tender Medallions *Skillet*

Rib Large End *Roast*
Rib Small End *Roast*
Rib Steak, Small End *Grill or Broil*
Ribeye Roast Boneless *Roast*
Ribeye Steak Boneless *Grill or Broil, Skillet*
Back Ribs *Grill or Broil*

Top Loin Steak Boneless *Grill or Broil*
T-Bone Steak *Grill or Broil*
Porterhouse Steak *Grill or Broil*
Tenderloin (Filet Mignon) *Roast*
Tenderloin Steak (Filet Mignon) *Grill or Broil*

Sirloin Steak, Flat Bone *Grill or Broil*
Sirloin Steak, Round Bone *Grill or Broil*
Top Sirloin Steak Boneless *Grill or Broil*
Tri-Tip *Roast*
Tri-Tip Steak *Grill or Broil*

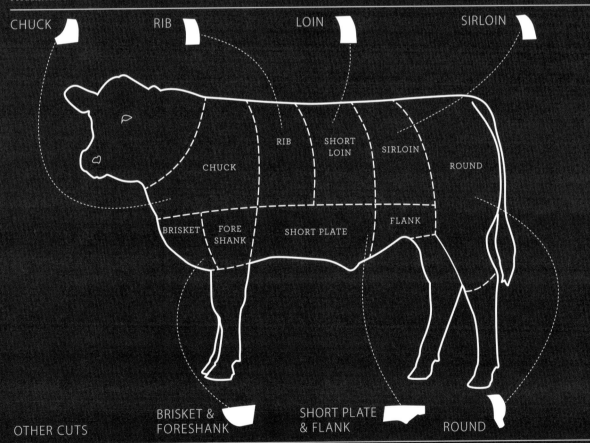

CHUCK RIB LOIN SIRLOIN

RIB
SHORT LOIN
CHUCK
SIRLOIN
ROUND

BRISKET FORE SHANK SHORT PLATE FLANK

BRISKET & FORESHANK SHORT PLATE & FLANK ROUND

OTHER CUTS

Beef *Stew*
Cubed Steak *Grill or Broil*
Beef for Kabobs *Grill or Broil*
Ground Beef Skillet, *Grill or Broil, Roast*

Brisket, Whole *Pot Roast*
Brisket, Flat Half *Pot Roast*
Brisket, Point Half *Pot Roast*
Shank Cross *Cut Stew*

Skirt Steak *Marinate & Grill or Broil*
Flank Steak *Marinate & Grill or Broil*

Round Steak Boneless *Marinate & Grill or Broil, Braise*
Bottom Round *Roast, Pot Roast*
Bottom Round Steak *Marinate & Grill or Broil, Braise*
Eye Round *Roast*
Eye Round Steak *Marinate & Grill or Broil*
Boneless Rump *Roast*
Tip *Roast*
Tip Steak *Skillet*

PORK CHART

Jowl *Braise, Cure, Smoke*

Smoked Cottage Roll *Broil*
Boston Style Butt *Roast, Braise, Smoke*
Blade Steaks *Braise*

Pork Tenderloin *Roast, Grill*
Sirloin Roast *Roast, Grill*
Loin Roast *Roast, Grill*

HEAD

SHOULDER

TOP LOIN

TOP LOIN

SHOULDER

HEAD

HAM

PICNIC HAM

BELLY

JOWL

JOWL

PICNIC HAM

BELLY

HAM

Jowl *Braise, Cure, Smoke*

Fresh Shoulder Hock *Braise, Roast*
Arm Steak *Braise*
Picnic Shoulder *Braise, Smoke, Cure*

Spare Ribs *Braise, Grill, Smoke*
Belly *Braise, Smoke, Cure*

Fresh Ham Roast *Braise, Roast*
Ham Steak *Braise*

LAMB CHART

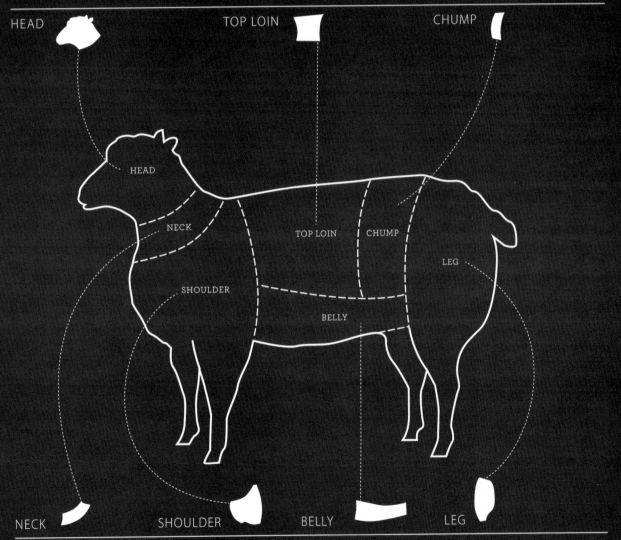

Lamb Chop *Roast, Grill*
Lamb Loin *Roast, Grill*
Lamb Cutlet *Pan Fry, Roast, Grill*

Boneless Chump Roast *Braise, Roast*
Chump Steaks *Braise, Roast*

Head *Braise, Smoke*

HEAD

TOP LOIN

CHUMP

HEAD

NECK

TOP LOIN

CHUMP

LEG

SHOULDER

BELLY

NECK

SHOULDER

BELLY

LEG

Neck Roll *Braise*

Whole Shoulder *Braise*
Shoulder Steaks *Roast, Braise*

Belly *Braise, Smoke*

Whole Leg *Braise*
Shank *Braise*
Top Leg Steaks *Braise*

ROASTING VEGETABLES

The chart below lists prep information and cooking times for many of the most common vegetables. For all, roast at 375°F.

The size of the dice or the whole vegetable will affect cooking time. Use this chart as a reference, but go by the color and tenderness of the vegetables to decide if they are done. For example, some asparagus spears are three times as thick as others and need to cook longer, and a spaghetti squash that is 2 pounds is going to cook faster than one that is 4 pounds.

Remember to oil and season your vegetables before roasting them, especially when they aren't being blanched or wet roasted. Many of these vegetables also work well with a higher cooking temp and shorter cooking time, but often they are sharing the oven with braising meats or other elements. The chart below is a good baseline to help you plan your meals.

VEGETABLE	SIZE AND PREP	TIME (MINUTES)	NOTES
ASPARAGUS	Whole	20–30	Remove the fibrous bottom third
BEETS	Whole in 2" water, covered	75–90	Peel and put in ice bath immediately after roasting
BELL PEPPERS	Whole	30–45 (flip every 15 minutes)	Adjust cooking time as needed for size
BROCCOLI	Medium florets, blanched	14–16	
BRUSSELS SPROUTS	Halved, blanched	35–45 (sliced side down)	Cook until very tender
CARROTS	Baby or 1" rounds	30–40	
CAULIFLOWER	Medium florets, blanched	35–45	
EGGPLANT	Peeled, 1" dice	20–30 (stir midway)	
FENNEL	½" slices	50–60 (flip once)	Keep fronds for finishing
GARLIC	Peeled, whole	20–25 (stir midway)	

VEGETABLE	SIZE AND PREP	TIME (MINUTES)	NOTES
GREENS, KALE	Washed and dried well, stemmed, and lightly coated with oil and salt	15+ (stir every 5 minutes)	Allow plenty of space between the leaves and cook until crispy
CHARD, OTHER GREENS	Washed and dried and lightly coated with oil and salt	15-20 (flip or stir midway)	
MUSHROOMS, BUTTON	Halved	20-30 (stir once)	
ONIONS (YELLOW OR RED)	½" slices or wedges	40-50 (flip or stir once)	
PARSNIPS	1" dice, blanched	35-45	
PLANTAINS	½" slices	30-40 (flip once)	
RADISHES	Halved or quartered	20-25	
RUTABAGA	½" dice	40-45 (stir midway)	
SPAGHETTI SQUASH	Halved and seeded in 1" water, sliced side down, covered	45-65	Cook until just tender in the center, not too soft
SUMMER SQUASH	1" dice or slices	30-40 (flip once)	
SUNCHOKES	½" slices	35-45 (flip once)	
SWEET POTATOES	½" dice	20-25	
TOMATOES, HALVED	Halved or quartered, sliced side up	45-60	
TOMATOES, DICED	½" dice	25-30	
TURNIPS	½" dice	40-45 (stir every 15 minutes)	
WINTER SQUASH	½" dice	40-45	
WINTER SQUASH FOR PUREE	Halved and seeded, in 1" water, sliced side down, covered	50-60	

COMMUNITY SUPPORTED AGRICULTURE

ALABAMA

FOREVER SUNRISE ORGANICS ●
(256) 282-1183
daveandroxanna@
foreversunriseorganics.com
www.foreversunriseorganics.com

BAD DUCK FARMS ●
Ragland, AL
marcus@badduckfarms.com
www.badduckfarms.com

AVARIETT BRANCH FARM ● ●
2796 Old Sylacauga Hwy.
Sylacauga, AL 35150
(256) 404-4088
www.averiettbranchfarmal.com

RANDLE FARMS ● ●
9215 Lee Road 54
Auburn, AL 36830
(334) 749-1073
www.randlefarms.net

ALASKA

ROSIE CREEK FARM ●
P.O. Box 106
Fairbanks, AK
csa@rosiecreekfarm
http://rosiecreekfarm.com

ARCTIC ORGANICS ●
1305 N. Smith Road
Palmer, AK 99645
(907) 746-1087
info@arcticorganics.com
www.arcticorganics.com

SUN CIRCLE FARM ● ●
5605 Farm Loop Road
Palmer, AK 99645
(907) 745-7406
ancokell@gmail.com
www.suncirclefarm.com

ARIZONA

BLUE SKY ORGANIC FARM ●
4762 N 189th Avenue
Litchfield Park, AZ 85340
(623) 266-4031
www.blueskyorganicfarms.com

DUNCAN FAMILY FARMS ●
18969 W. McDowell Road
Buckeye, AZ 85396
(623) 853-9880
saladadaytheduncanway.com

TUCSON COMMUNITY SUPPORTED
AGRICULTURE ● ●
(520) 203-1010
tucsoncsa@tucsoncsa.org
www.tucsoncsa.org

DOUBLE CHECK RANCH ●
4965 N. Camino Rio
Winkelman, AZ 85292
(520) 357-6515
www.doublecheckranch.com

ARKANSAS

SYCAMORE BEND FARM ●
875 CR 3025
Eureka Springs, AR 72632
(479) 981-3128

NORTH PULASKI FARM ●
13018 Ellen Cv
Cabot, AR 72023
(501) 240-4233
www.northpulaskifarms.com

FOSTER'S FOUR SEASONS FARM ● ●
1211 Highway 300
Houston, AR 72070
(501) 563-4645

WHITTON FARMS ● ●
5157 W St Hwy 118
Tyronza, AR 72386
(870) 815-9519
www.whittonfarms.com

CALIFORNIA

INLAND EMPIRE CSA ●
(951) 693-0272
info@inlandempirecsa.com
www.inlandempirecsa.com

SUZIE'S FARM ●
2570 Sunset Avenue
San Diego, CA 92154
(619) 662-1780
http://suziesfarm.com

BLUE HOUSE FARM ●
5000 Pescadero Creek Road.
Pescadero, CA 94060
(650) 879-0704
www.bluehouseorganicfarm.com

EATING WITH THE SEASONS ● ●
(third-party CSA service for
northern California)
customerservice@eatwiththeseasons.com
(831) 245-8125
www.eatwiththeseasons.com

OPEN SPACES MEATS ●
Newman, CA 95360
(209) 262-8780
http://openspacemeats.com

COLORADO

FARM SHARE/COMMUNITY SUPPORTED AGRICULTURE PROGRAMS IN COLORADO ✚
http://coloradocsas.info/csas/browseFullList

FIELD TO FORK CSA ●
P.O. Box 301
Palisade, CO 81526
(970) 216-2642
Fieldtoforkcsa@gmail.com
www.fieldtoforkcsa.com

INDIAN RIDGE FARM AND BAKERY ● ●
P.O. Box 963
1401 County Road 43ZN
Norwood, CO 81423
(970) 327-0336
daranyi@rmi.net
http://indianridgefarm.org

MONROE ORGANIC FARMS, LLC. ● ●
25525 Weld County Road 48
Kersey, CO 80644
(970) 284-7941
www.monroefarm.com

EASTERN PLAINS NATURAL FOOD CO-OP ●
P.O. Box 224
Bennett, CO 80102
(303) 644-4079
co_op@easternplains.com
http://easternplains.com

CONNECTICUT

JOE'S GARDEN ● ●
109 Leigus Road
Wallingford, CT 06492
(203) 265-0696
info@farmerjoesgardens.com
www.farmerjoesgardens.com

DELAWARE

EVANS FARMS PRODUCE ●
9843 Seashore Highway
Bridgeville, DE 19933
(302) 337-8130
EvansFarmLLC@gmail.com
www.evansfarmsproduce.com

FIFER ORCHARDS ●
1919 Allabands Mill Road
Camden-Wyoming, DE 19934
(302) 697-2141
www.fiferorchards.com

HIGHLAND ORCHARDS FARM MARKET ● ●
7460 Old Lancaster Pike
Hockessin, DE 19707
(302)239-4915
henrettysmarket@gmail.com
http://highlandorchardsfarmmarket.com

JUBILEE BACK FORTY ● ●
29055 Deer Haven Lane
Milton DE 19968
(302) 542-9642
www.jubileebackforty.com

FLORIDA

KAI KAI FARM ●
8006 SW Kanner Highway
Indiantown, FL 34956
(772) 597-1717
kaikaifarm@hotmail.com
www.kaikaifarm.com

SWEETWATER ORGANIC COMMUNITY FARM ●
6942 W. Comanche Ave
Tampa, FL 33634
(813) 887-4066
info@sweetwater-organic.org
http://sweetwater-organic.org

SCOOBY'S FARM ●
704 Barnes Road
Monticello, FL 32344
(954) 639-3666
http://scoobysfarm.us

CIRCLE C FARM ●
951 Morris Taylor Road
Felda, FL 33930-0262
(239) 776-9054
www.Sheep-Life.com

GEORGIA

RISING FAWN GARDENS ●
315 Cureton Mill Road
Rising Fawn, GA 30738
(423) 991-1188
www.risingfawngardens.com

EAST OF EDEN FARMS ● ●
1223 Taylorsville Macedonia Road
Taylorsville, GA 30178
(678) 641-2042
www.eastofedenfarms.com

BROAD RIVER PASTURES ● ●
Elberton, GA
(706) 283-7946
www.BroadRiverPastures.com

HAWAII

KAHUMANA ORGANIC FARM & CAFE ●
86-660 Lualualei Homestead Road
Waianae, HI 96792
(808) 696-8844
http://kahumanafarms.org

OHIA FIELDS FARM ● ●
41-1679 Niupea Homestead Road
Ookala, HI 96734
(808) 345-8248
sites.google.com/site/ohiafieldsfarm

KULA FIELDS FARMSHOP ● ●
(808) 280-2099
http://kulafields.com

IDAHO

CREATE COMMON GOOD FARM ●
4750 S. Surprise Way
Boise, ID 83716
(410) 279-9829
www.createcommongood.org

THE JENKINS CLAN ●
Nampa, ID 83652
thejenkinsclan@q.com
www.producebythejenkinsclan.com

GREENTREE NATURALS ●
2003 Rapid Lightning Road
Sandpoint, ID 83864
www.greentreenaturals.com

CASCADE CREEK FARM ●
5261 Westside Road
Bonners Ferry, ID 83805
(208) 267-1325
http://cascadecreekfarm.com

ILLINOIS

HARVEST MOON FARMS CSA ●
3354 North Paulina St., Suite 200
Chicago, IL 60657
(773) 472-7950
info@harvestmoon-farms.com
www.harvestmoon-farms.com

✚ DIRECTORY
● PRODUCE
● ● PRODUCE AND LIVESTOCK
● LIVESTOCK

BEAVER CREEK GARDENS CSA ●
20506 Beaverton Road
Poplar Grove, IL 61065
(815) 494-1251
Beavercreekgardens.com

BROAD BRANCH FARM ● ●
15848 Twp Rd 500 N
Wyoming, IL 61491
(309) 231-9290
(309) 231-9280
broadbranchfarm@gmail.com
www.broadbranchfarm.com

GREEN EARTH FARM ● ●
8308 Barnard Mill Road
Richmond, IL 60071
(815) 351-6357
www.greenearthfarm.org

INDIANA

BECKER FARMS ● ●
7392 N Wilbur Wright Road
Mooreland, IN 47360
(765) 714-4457
www.beckerfarmsin.com

SILVERTHORN FARM ● ●
4485 W 1000N
Rossville, IN 46065
(765) 230-0735
www.silverthorn-farm.com

FARMING ENGINEERS ● ●
3500 S CR 1380 E
Kirklin, IN 46050
(317) 836-5061
burkefarm.wordpress.com

IOWA

ABBE HILLS FARM CSA ● ●
825 Abbe Hills Road
Mt. Vernon, IA 52314
(319) 895-6924
www.abbehills.com

BLUE GATE FARM ● ●
749 Wyoming St
Chariton, IA 50049
(641) 203-0758
www.bluegatefarmfresh.com

+ DIRECTORY
● PRODUCE
● ● PRODUCE AND LIVESTOCK
● LIVESTOCK

GENUINE FAUX FARM ● ●
P.O. Box 121
Tripoli, IA 50676
www.genuinefauxfarm.com

KANSAS

CRUM'S HEIRLOOMS, LLC ●
16211 Stillwell Road
Bonner Springs, KS 66012
(913) 422-1630

HOME GROWN KANSAS! LLC ●
Wichita, KS
(316) 207-6915
homegrownkansas.com

MORNING HARVEST FARM ● ●
8933 NE 72nd St
Walton, KS 67151
(316) 303-7118
www.morningharvestfarm.com

KENTUCKY

BERRIES ON BRYAN STATION ●
4744 Bryan Station
Lexington, KY 40516
(859) 293-0077
http://berriesonbryanstation.com

TRIPLE J FARM ● ●
2287 Long Lick Road
Georgetown, KY 40324
(502) 863-6786
http://triplejfarm.org/

ELMWOOD STOCK FARM ● ●
Georgetown, KY
(859) 621-0755
www.elmwoodstockfarm.com

LOUISIANA

INGLEWOOD FARM ● ●
6233 Old Baton Rouge Hwy
Alexandria, LA 71302
(318) 442-6398
www.inglewoodfarm.com

GOTREAUX FAMILY FARMS ● ●
205 Facile Road
Scott, LA 70583
(337) 873-0383
www.gofamilyfarms.com

BUTTERFIELD FARMS ●
228 Butterfield Lane
Pollock, LA 71467
(318) 899-5789
www.butterfieldfarms.net

MAINE

ALMA FARM ● ●
488 Spec Pond Road
Porter, ME 04068
(207) 831-1088
www.almafarm.com

WILLOW POND FARM ● ●
395 Middle Road
Sabattus, ME 04280-6662
(207) 375-6662
www.willowpf.com

NO VIEW FARM & BAKERY ● ●
855 South Rumford Road
Rumford, ME 04276
(207) 364-1080
www.noviewfarm.com

MARYLAND

EVERMORE FARM ●
150 Rockland Road
Westminster, MD 21158
(443) 398-6548
evermorefarm.com

ONE STRAW FARM ●
19718 Kirkwood Shop Road
White Hall, MD 21161
(410) 343-1828
www.onestrawfarm.com

ROUSEDALE FARM ● ●
2604 Fallston Road
Fallston, MD 21047
www.rousedalefarm.com

MASSACHUSETTS

APPONAGANSETT FARM ● ●
607 Elm Street
South Dartmouth, MA 02748
(774) 400-7277
www.apponagansettfarm.com

FARMER DAVE'S CSA ● ●
437 Parker Road
Dracut, MA 01826
(978) 349-1952
www.farmerdaves.net

THE HERB HILL MICRODAIRY ● ●
320 High Plain Road
Andover, MA 01810
(978) 475-7931
www.theherbhillmicrodairy.mckain.me

COPPERHEAD FARM ●
4 East Street
Hadley, MA 01035
(413) 559-7713
www.copperheadfarm.com

MICHIGAN

FARMER DAVE'S ●
437 Parker Road
Dracut, MA 01826
(978) 349-1952
farm@farmerdaves.net

NELSFARM PRODUCE ● ●
14675 28 Mile Road
Albion, MI 49224
(517) 629-5472
nelsfarmproduce.com

EAST RIVER ORGANIC FARM
440 N. Wheeler Road
Snover, MI 48472
(810) 404-1723
www.eastriverorganic.com

MINNESOTA

CSA FARM DIRECTORY 2013 ✚
http://landstewardshipproject.
org/repository/1/745/csa_
directory_2013_2_14_13.pdf

SHEPHERD FLOCK FARM ●
Terry Arnold
16987 260th St.
Lindstrom, MN 55045
(651) 257-2656
jtarnold@frontiernet.net

BOSSY ACRES ●
P.O. Box 7250
Minneapolis, MN 5407
bossy-acres@hotmail.com

TREASURED HAVEN FARM ● ●
53407 Government Road
Rush City, MN 55069
(320) 358-3581
csa@treasuredhavenfarm.com
www.treasuredhavenfarm.com

SIMPLE HARVEST FARM ● ●
9800 155th Street East
Nerstrand, MN 55053
(507) 664-9446
kzeman@kmwb.net
www.simpleharvestfarm.com

TRUE COST FARM ●
Montrose, MN
(612) 568-4686
info@truecostfarm.com
www.truecostfarm.com

MISSISSIPPI

UNCLE BUBBA'S FARM ●
2050 Adams Station Road
Utica, MS 39175
(601) 473-9183
www.unclebubbasfarm.com

STEEDE FARMS ● ●
140 Hwy 63 South
Lucedale, MS 39452
(601) 508-1372
www.steedefarms.com

LEVEE RUN FARM ● ●
802 Grenada Blvd. Ext.
Greenwood, MS 38930
(662) 392-4189
leveerunfarm.org

MISSOURI

KANSAS CITY FOOD CIRCLE
(third-party CSA service) ● ●
(913) 620-8427
www.KCFoodCircle.org

MILLSAP FARM ● ●
6593 North Emu Lane
Springfield, MO 65803
(417) 839-0847
www.millsapfarms.com

DANJO FARMS ● ●
1210 Private Road 2717
Moberly, MO 65270
(573) 823-5452
www.danjofarms.com

OUR CITY FARM ● ●
4539 Delmar Blvd
St. Louis, MO 63108
(314) 282-5290
www.ourcityfarm.com

MONTANA

GALLATIN VALLEY BOTANICAL ●
34651 Frontage Road
Bozeman, MT 59715
(406) 599-2361
www.gallatinvalleybotanical.com

WHOLESOME FOODS ● ●
2161 Hwy 310
Bridger, MT 59014
(406) 596-0492
montanawholesomefoods.com

GROUNDWORKS FARM ● ●
8 Clark Street
Fort Shaw, MT 59443
groundworksfarmmt.com

NEBRASKA

ROBINETTE FARMS ● ●
17675 SW 14th Street
Martell, NE 68404
(402) 794-4025
robinettefarms.com

WENNINGHOFF ● ●
6707 Wenninghoff Road
Omaha, NE 68122
(402) 571-2057
www.wenninghoff.com

COMMON GOOD FARM ● ●
17201 NW 40th St.
Raymond, NE 68428
www.commongoodfarm.com

SUNNY SLOPE FARM ● ●
22876 S. 94th Road
Filley, NE 68357
(402) 223-9541
picasaweb.google.com/mfriesen2

NEVADA

QUAIL HOLLOW FARM ● ●
P.O. Box 688
Overton, NV 89040
(702) 397-2021
quailhollowfarm@mvdsl.com

CUSTOM GARDENS ORGANIC
PRODUCE FARM AND CSA ● ●
3701 Elm Street
Silver Springs, NV 89429
(775) 577-2069
www.customgardens-organic-farm.com

MEADOW VALLEY CSA FARM ● ●
1012 E. McKnightt Ave.
Las Vegas, NV 89025
(702) 864-2291
www.meadowvalleycsa.com

NEW HAMPSHIRE

LEDGE TOP FARM ●
487 Lyndeborough Center Road
Wilton, NH 03086
(603) 654-6002
ledgetopfarm.com

HAINES HILL FARM ● ●
336 Haines Hill Road
Wolfeboro, NH 03894
(603) 569-1936
haineshillfarm.com

STEVE NORMANTON ● ●
226 Charles Bancroft Hwy
Litchfield, NH 03052
(603) 320-1169
www.stevenormanton.com

NEW JERSEY

MUTH FAMILY FARM ●
1639 Pitman Downer Road
Williamstown, NJ 08094
(856) 582-0363
www.muthfamilyfarm.com

GOOD TREE FARM ● ●
82 Jacobstown Road
New Egypt, NJ 08533
(609) 672-2080
manager@goodtreefarms.com

GREEN DUCHESS FARM ● ●
289 Bennets Lane
Franklin Township, NJ 08873
(973) 602-7376
greenduchessfarm.com

NEW MEXICO

BENEFICIAL FARMS CSA ●
P.O. Box 30044
Santa Fe, NM 87592
(505) 470-1969
www.beneficialfarm.com

LAS PALOMAS HEIRLOOM FARMS ●
625 Las Palomas Canyon Road
Williamsburg, NM 87942
(575) 635-1690
palomasfarm.com

RED HOT POKER FARMS ● ●
PO Box 4301
Roswell, NM 88202
(505) 400-8736
redhotpokerfarms.com

PAGE RIVER BOTTOM FARM ●
17780 E. Vino Ave.
Reedley, CA 93654-9702
(559) 638-3124
www.pageriverbottomfarm.com

NEW YORK

JUST FOOD: CSA IN NYC ✚
http://www.justfood.org/csa

FOUR WINDS FARM ● ●
158 Marabac Road
Gardiner, NY 12525
(845) 255-3088
www.bestweb.net/~fourwind

● SEAFOOD
✚ DIRECTORY
● PRODUCE
● ● PRODUCE AND LIVESTOCK
● LIVESTOCK

GRINDSTONE FARM ● ●
780 Co. Rt 28 Tinker Tavern Road
Pulaski, NY 13142
(315) 298-4139
www.GrindstoneFarm.com

OTTER HOOK FARMS MEAT CSA ● ●
223 McCafferty Road
Greenville, NY 12083
(518) 239-6049
otterhookfarms.com

LUCKI 7 LIVESTOCK CO. ●
Rte #69
Rodman, NY 13682
(845) 757-5591
www.lucki7livestock.com

NORTH CAROLINA

CIRCLE ACRES FARM ●
P.O. Box 119
Siler City, NC 27344
(919) 200-9741
circleacres.info

CANE CREEK ASPARAGUS &
COMPANY CSA ●
P. O. Box 2012
Fairview, NC 28730
www.CaneCreekCSA.com

MILL RIVER FARM ● ●
731 Cain Road
Mt Airy, NC 27030
(336) 351-0935
millriverfarm.com

FARM TO FORK MEAT ● ●
(third-party CSA service)
2800-142 Sumner Blvd.
Raleigh, NC 27616
(919) 606-0320
www.farmtoforkmeat.com

NORTH DAKOTA

RIVERBOUND FARM ●
2175 53rd Street
Mandan, ND 58554
(701) 202-9834
riverboundfarm.com

LLAMA TRAX GARDENS ● ●
3925 115th Ave SE
Valley City , ND 58072
(701) 845-1191
llamatraxgardens.com

TURTLE COVE FARM ● ●
14838 57th St NW
Williston, ND 58801
(701) 875-4341
www.turtlecovefarm.com

OHIO

MURRAY HILL FARM ● ●
5761 Ferry Road
Wakeman, OH 44889
(419) 929-5157
www.murrayhillfarm.com

TERRAVITA FARMS ● ●
3774 Chestnut Hills Road
Newark, OH 43055
www.terravitafarms.com/Welcome.html

FINN MEADOWS FARM ● ●
8100 Perin Road
Cincinnati, OH 45242
(812) 212-1196
www.finnmeadowsfarm.com

OKLAHOMA

TG FARMS ●
1580 N.W. Hwy 37
Newcastle, OK 73065
(405) 387-3276
www.tgfarms.com

THREE SPRINGS FARM ●
P.O. Box 13
Oaks, OK 74359
(918) 868-5450
www.threespringsfarm.com

HEAVEN SENT FOOD & FIBER ● ●
401 E Downing St
Tahlequah, OK 74464
(918) 431-4774
HeavenSentFoodandFiber.com

OREGON

PORT ORFORD SUSTAINABLE
SEAFOOD ●
444 Jackson Street
Port Orford, OR 97465
(541) 332-0627
posustainableseafood.com

RISING STONE FARM ●
Portland, OR 97213
(503) 916-9576
farmers@risingstonefarm.com

HELIOS FARMS ● ●
2077 Skelly South
Yoncalla, OR 97499
(541) 908-0561
www.heliosfarms.com

PENNSYLVANIA

JACK'S FARM ●
1370 West Schuylkill Road
Pottstwon, PA 19465
(610) 413-9088
jacksfarm@gmail.com
http://jacksfarm.net

GREENSGROW FARMS ● ●
2501 East Cumberland St.
Philadelphia, PA 19125
(215) 380-4355
csa@greengrows.org

HICKORY RIDGE NATURAL
HARVEST CSA ● ●
668 Strongs Road
Irvona, PA 16656
(814) 672-3009
www.hrnaturalharvest.com

RHODE ISLAND

BLAZING STAR FARM ●
P.O. Box 1225
Block Island, RI 02807
(401) 466-5797
blazingstarfarm.com

STONYLEDGE FARM ● ●
107 Kuehn Road
Hopkinton, RI 02804
(401) 377-4514
www.studiofarmproducts.com

CASEY FARM ● ●
2325 Boston Neck Road
Saunderstown, RI 02874
(401) 295-1030
www.historicnewengland.org/visit/
homes/casey.htm

SOUTH CAROLINA

SUGARFOOT ORGANIC FARMS ●
Hwy. 701 N.
Conway, SC 29526
darel@sugarfootfarms.com

CITY ROOTS ● ●
1005 Airport Blvd.
Columbia, SC 29205
(803) 254-2302
www.cityroots.org

LEGARE FARMS ● ●
2620 Hanscombe Pt. Road
Johns Island, SC 29455
(843) 559-0788
www.legarefarms.org

SOUTH DAKOTA

LINDA'S GARDENS ●
24009 465th Ave
Chester, SD 57016
(605) 489-2651
www.lindasgardens.com

THE GOOD EARTH ●
28318 466th Avenue (Hwy 17)
Lennox, SD 57039
(605) 929-7394
www.thegoodearth.us

COTEAU SUNRISE FARM ● ●
42499 109th St
Britton, SD 57430
(605) 448-5901
coteausunrisefarm.com

TENNESSEE

WILSON FAMILY FARM ●
Powell, TN
(865) 947-1449

WILD THINGS FARM ●
Crab Orchard, TN
www.wildthingscsafarm.com

WATERS ORGANIC FARM ●
Baxter, TN
(931) 267-9242

ALLENBROOKE FARMS ●
Spring Hill, TN
(615) 406-4592
www.allenbrookefarms.com

WALNUT HILLS FARM ●
Bethpage, TN
(615) 374-4575
www.walnuthillsfarm.com

WISNER FARMS ●
Dandridge, TN
(865) 397-2512
wisnerfarms.moonfruit.com

TEXAS

COMEBACK CREEK FARM ●
Dallas, TX
www.comebackcreek.com

BIG BLUE SKY FARM ●
Austin, TX 78704
(512) 538-5487

BURRO MALO FARM ●
(512) 964-0350
Adamsville, TX 76550

EPPS FAMILY FARM ● ●
10383 Jim Towns Lane
Calvert, TX 77837
(979) 224 3453
eppsfamilyplanters.com

HOME SWEET FARM ● ●
Brenham, TX
(979) 251-9922
www.homesweetfarm.com

COLD SPRINGS FARM CSA ● ●
Weatherford, TX
site.coldspringsfarmcsa.com

UTAH

LA NAY FERME ●
Provo, UT
lanayferme.com

HEARTLAND FARMS CSA ●
(435) 619-4250
myheartlandfarms.com

WESTOVER FAMILY FARMS ● ●
620 S 500 W
Vernal, UT 84078-4303
(435) 789-8808

NEW DAWN FARMS ● ●
(801) 390-1265
www.newdawnfarm.com

APPENZELL FARM ● ●
1146 East 4400 North
Hyde Park, UT 84318
(435) 535-1121
appenzellfarm.com

CHRISTIANSEN'S FAMILY FARM ●
175 E. Sharp Road
Vernon, UT 84080
(435) 839-3482
www.ChristiansenFarm.com

VERMONT

GOOD EATS CSA ● ●
266 S. Craftsbury Road
Craftsbury, VT 05826
(802) 586-2882 x 6
goodeats@petesgreens.com
www.petesgreens.com

FULL MOON FARM ● ●
2083 Gilman Road
Hinesburg, VT 05461
(802) 598-1986
info@fullmoonfarminc.com
www.fullmoonfarminc.com

VIRGINIA

FREDERICKSBURG AREA CSA
PROJECT (FACSAP) ●
Hurkamp Park
Fredericksburg, VA 22401
FACSAP@yahoo.com
facsap.wordpress.com

POTOMAC VEGETABLE FARMS ●
9627 Leesburg Pike
Vienna, VA 22182
www.potomacvegetablefarms.com

WHITE FLINT FARM ● ●
(434) 791-3773
whiteflintfarm@gmail.com
www.whiteflintfarm.com

DENDI RANCH ● ●
650 Trottinridge Road
Clarksville, VA 23927
(434) 374-2998

BULL RUN MOUNTAIN FARM ● ●
4360 Highpoint Ln
The Plains, VA 20198
www.bullrunfarm.com

BRIGHTWOOD VINEYARD AND
FARM ● ●
1202 Lillards Ford Road
Brightwood, VA 22715
(540) 948-6845
www.brightwoodvineyardandfarm.com

BELLE MEADE FARM ●
353 F.T. Valley Rd.
Sperryville, VA 22740
(540) 987-9748
www.bellemeade.net

CHICAMA RUN ●
14809 Purcellville Road
Purcellville, VA 20132
(540) 668-9828
www.chicamarun.com

TUCKAHOE LAMB AND CATTLE
COMPANY ●
989 Cartersville Road
Cartersville, VA 23027
(804) 506-4015
www.tuckahoeplantationlivestock.com

WASHINGTON

BOISTFORT VALLEY FARM ●
426 Boistfort Road
Curtis, WA 98538
(360) 245-3796
info@BoistfortValleyFarm.com
www.boistfortvalleyfarm.com

HEAVENLY HILLS HARVEST ●
764 South Emerald Road
Sunnyside, WA 98944
(509) 840-5600
www.heavenlyhillsharvest.com

FOXDOG FARM ●
26096 Miller Bay Road NE, PO Box
1330
Kingston, WA 98346
(360) 297-7135
www.foxdogfarm.com

DOG MOUNTAIN FARM ● ●
7026 Tolt Highlands Road NE
Carnation, WA 98014
(425) 333-0833
www.dogmtnfarm.com

HIGH ROOST RANCH ●
128 Mount Adams Hwy.
Glenwood, WA 98619
(509) 364-3312
highroostranch.wordpress.com

WEST VIRGINIA

ROUND RIGHT FARM ● ●
145 Dream Field Ln
Terra Alta, WV 26764
(304) 789-5887
roundrightfarm@gmail.com

FRESH AND LOCAL CSA ●
P.O. Box 3047
Shepherdstown, WV 25443
(306) 876-3382
grassfinished@freshandlocalcsa.com
http://www.freshandlocalcsa.com

WISCONSIN

CSA FARM DIRECTORY 2013 ✚
http://landstewardshipproject.
org/repository/1/745/csa_
directory_2013_2_14_13.pdf

FAIRSHARE CSA COALITION ✚
http://www.csacoalition.org

HOG'S BACK FARM ●
W8937 Moritz Lane
Arkansaw, WI 54721
(612) 756-0690
david@hogsbackfarm.com
www.hogsbackfarm.com

HUNGRY TURTLE FARM &
LEARNING CENTER ● ●
410 125th Street
Amery, WI 54001
(715) 268-4214
kmerton@hungryturtle.net
www.hungryturtle.net

EENER'S FARM ● ●
N12449 220th St.
Boyceville, WI 54725
(715) 643-2803
eenermachine@gmail.com
www.eenersfarm.blogspot.com

WYOMING

CLEAR CREEK VALLEY PRODUCE ●
4312 US Highway 14/16 East
Clearmont, WY 82835
(307) 758-4391

FERTILE GROUNDS ●
(570) 262-3930
Fertile.Grounds.Office@gmail.com
www.fertilegroundscsa.com

MEADOW MAID FOODS, LLC ● ●
P.O. Box 164
Yoder, WY 82244
(307) 534-2289
cindyr@meadowmaidfoods.com

HEART MOUNTAIN VALLEY RANCH
100% ORGANIC ●
27 Lane 19
Cody, WY 82414
(307) 587-8514

✚ DIRECTORY
● PRODUCE
● ● PRODUCE AND LIVESTOCK
● LIVESTOCK

ACKNOWLEDGMENTS

Mom and Dad: Good job. Seriously, I could not have been more fortunate in my parents. You gave me intelligence, thoughtfulness, and empathy. What else could a good man need?

Sarah: I think there's a restaurant in some far-off city that's short a chef right now thanks to you. Thanks for helping me find the path that led here. I love you.

The chefs: Bies, Eb, Ryan, Linton, Charles, Johnny, Irwin, Bruce, Knight, Diehl, Johnson, Kanadu, Dahl, Mekolites, Brock, Chang, Bryant, Keller, and so many more, until Escoffier and Careme. I am standing on all of your shoulders. Thank you.

The cooks: Starting with Orlando, who, instead of ignoring the *blanquito*, taught me Spanish and how to work fast, and everyone after. Thanks for making me better.

Simone, our book assistant, stylist, and recorder: It would not have gotten done without you.

My brothers: Thanks for being my brothers.

And to everyone in the Paleo world, including but not limited to Diane, Bill and Hayley, Liz, Tony of course, and many, many more: Thank you for welcoming us.

SPRING

34
Brined and Roasted Chicken with Cider Pan Sauce

36
Blood Orange Glazed Pork Chops

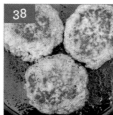
38
Classic Burgers

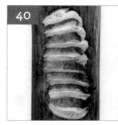
40
Pan-Seared Duck Breast

42
Panang Duck Curry

44
Pork Loin Wrapped in Bacon

46
Battered Fish Tacos

48
Fried Cauliflower Rice

50
Mango Cauliflower Sticky Rice

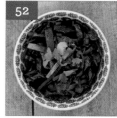
52
Spicy Cabbage Slaw

54
Roasted Carrot Puree

56
Carrot Pistou

58
Grilled Artichoke and Shiitake Mushroom Salad with Roasted Garlic

60
Arugula, Strawberry, and Radish Salad with Balsamic Vinaigrette

62
Shaved Asparagus and Beet Salad

64
Bacon and Shaved Brussels Sprouts Salad

66
Carrot Lemongrass Soup

SUMMER

72
Cherry Braised
Lamb Shoulder

74
Burgers with Avocado
Salsa

76
Ground Elk Patties
with Spinach and Sweet
Potato

78
Meatballs with
Zucchini Noodles and
Peach Basil Salsa

80
Thai Ginger Pork
Sausage

82
Pork Pastor

84
Poached Sea Bass
with Pan-Seared Maitake, Bok
Choy, and Daikon Noodles

88
Stuffed Anaheim
Chiles

90
Pulled Creole Braised
Chicken

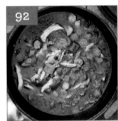
92
Okra Brunswick Stew

94
Shrimp with Grapes
and Zucchini Noodles

96
Beer Butt Chicken

98
Braised Pork
and Barbecue Sauce

100
Garlicky Burgers
over Sweet Potato Hash

102
Collard Greens

104
Artichoke, Olive,
and Tomato Dip

106
Eggplant Dip

108
Burst Tomato Sauce

110
Smashed Plantains

112
Egg and Fruit Hash

114
Grilled Avocado,
Portobello, and Red
Onion Salad

116
Grilled Cantaloupe
and Eggplant Salad

118
Fennel and Tomato
Salad

120
Coffee Ice Cream

122
Mango Ice Cream

COOKING THROUGH A CSA BOX

130 Cast Iron Charred Broccolini

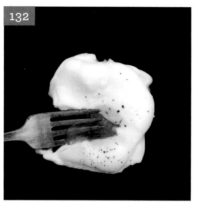

132 Poached Eggs

134 Romaine, Radish, and Roasted Beet Salad

136 Bison Roulade with Pan-Wilted Chard

140 Roasted Acorn Squash with Fresh Sage

142 Anaheim Chile and Apple Salad

FALL

148 Coq au Vin

150 Oven-Braised Ribs

152 Pork Belly

154 Beg Alicha (Stewed Lamb with Cardamom)

156 Beg Wot (Stewed Lamb with Berbere)

157 Atkilt (Spiced Vegetable Stew)

158 Brined and Pan-Seared Pork Chops

160 Spaghetti Squash Mexicana

162 Mushroom Ragout with Gremolata

164 Cauliflower Dumplings

165 Pumpkin Dumplings

168 Romanesco and Sweet Potatoes

170 Chive Mashed Potatoes

172 Roasted Fall Squash

174 Roasted Butternut Squash with Currants

176 Roasted Spaghetti Squash

178 Sautéed Black Trumpet Mushrooms

180 Chicken Pho

182 Chowchow

184 Quick Kim Chi

186 Chocolate Pumpkin Seeds

187 Coconut Curry Pumpkin Seeds

190 Chocolate Pumpkin Pie

WINTER

Braised Lamb

Lamb Scramble

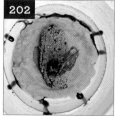
Lamb Quenelles

Lamb Meatballs

Bison Bolognese

Cornish Game Hen and Roulades

Braised Short Ribs with Fennel and Sous Vide Carrots

Strip Steak

Celeriac Puree

Roasted Beets with Salsify and Fennel Fronds

Oil-Poached Salsify

Cast Iron Wilted Kale

Glazed Sweet Potatoes

New Potatoes with Kale

Braised Cipollini

Herb-Roasted Beets

Beet Puree & Beet Gratin

Celery Root Salad

Sweet Potato and Apple Salad

Candied Bacon and Apple Salad

Braised Lamb and Kale Salad

CONDIMENTS

248
Ketchup

250
Mustard

252
Chimichurri Sauce

254
Arugula Pesto

256
Baconnaise

260
Truffle Mayonnaise

260
Duck Fat Mayonnaise

262
Marinara Sauce

264
Balsamic Vinaigrette

266
Bone Marrow
Vinaigrette

STOCKS

270
Hearty Chicken Stock

272
Shrimp Stock or Broth

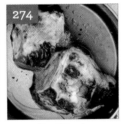
274
Beef Stock

276
Pho Broth

RECIPE INDEX

INDEX